Eyewitness
Soldier

First-aid kit

Military bugle

Jungle camouflage jacket

Photo of a loved one

US Army colonel's badge

Poppy

Roman armor

AK47 assault rifle

POW glasses

Service medals

Eyewitness
Soldier

Written by
SIMON ADAMS

Siege tower

Early Chinese rockets

AS90 self-propelled artillery

Zulu shield

Civil War ambulance

DK

DK Publishing

Roman
centurion's
helmet

King's shilling

Night-vision
goggles

DK

LONDON, NEW YORK,
MELBOURNE, MUNICH, AND DELHI

Consultant Andrew Robertshaw

Senior editor Rob Houston
Senior art editor Alison Gardner
Managing editor Camilla Hallinan
Managing art editor Owen Peyton Jones
Art director Martin Wilson
Associate Publisher Andrew Macintyre
Picture researcher Louise Thomas
Production editor Andy Hilliard
Senior production controller Pip Tinsley

Tall Tree Ltd.
Editors Rob Colson, David John,
Claudia Martin, and Jon Richards
Designers Ben Ruocco, Ed Simkins,
and Jonathan Vipond
Indexer Chris Bernstein

Sword fighting positions

Beretta Model
92FS pistol

Field cutlery

US Marine
Corps badge

First published in the United States in 2009 by
DK Publishing, 375 Hudson Street, New York, New York 10014

Copyright © 2009 Dorling Kindersley Limited

09 10 11 12 13 10 9 8 7 6 5 4 3 2 1
ED743 – 12/08

A catalog record for this book is available from the Library of Congress.

ISBN 978-0-7566-4539-7 (HC); 978-0-7566-4540-3 (ALB)

Color reproduction by Colourscan, Singapore.
Printed and bound by Toppan Printing Co. (Shenzen) Ltd., China

Portable fuel and matches

Discover more at
www.dk.com

Wood alcohol

Rigid raider

Contents

Hand grenades

The soldier

A SOLDIER IS a professional fighter: a man—or woman—who is paid to fight for a country or a cause. A soldier is drawn from among the civilian, or unarmed, population, and is specially trained to fight. He joins an army, wears a uniform, and serves for anything from a couple of years to a lifetime. Soldiers have existed throughout human history, ever since peoples first began to fight one another for food, land, status, or superiority. A soldier's life is hard, since he must be fit and ready to fight at a moment's notice in difficult and often dangerous circumstances. Yet a soldier's life may also be extraordinarily varied and exciting.

PATRIOTISM
A soldier's first loyalty is often to his country and its flag, such as the flag of the Russian Federation, above. The Chinese People's Liberation Army is currently the largest army in the world, with 2.3 million troops. Twenty-one of 193 countries in the world have no army, including Iceland, Costa Rica, and many small Caribbean and Pacific island states.

Kabuto (helmet) carries warrior's personal crest

Japanese samurai warrior

Banner of the warrior's lord

Kote (armored sleeve) and sode (shoulder guard) protect the arm

SELF-DEFENSE
Soldiers are often used to defend their nation from attack. In medieval times, European soldiers often defended walled towns or castles that were under threat. These English soldiers were in action in 1204 when Rouen in Normandy was besieged by French forces.

PERSONAL LOYALTY
Soldiers can sometimes fight out of personal loyalty to a local lord or political master, particularly in a country where there is civil war and central authority has broken down. In the medieval world, the samurai warriors of Japan and the knights of western Europe owed their loyalty to the lords who employed them rather than to the emperor or king who ruled them.

Soldiers of the People's Liberation Army

Haidate (lower thigh) and suneate (shin) armor protect the leg

DISCIPLINE
The most important lesson a soldier must learn is discipline. Without discipline, a soldier might disobey or ignore orders and endanger his own life or those of his comrades. These Chinese soldiers are learning the essential discipline of marching in straight ranks with their rifles held out in front of them. One wrong step, and the bayonet attached to the rifle behind you could stab you in the back.

INFANTRY AND CAVALRY

Historically, soldiers have been divided between infantry (those who fight on foot) and cavalry (those who fight on horseback). The two often fought alongside or against each other. The Russian Imperial Guard cavalry and French infantry met in this engagement at Austerlitz, in the present-day Czech Republic, in 1805. Today, horses have been replaced by armored vehicles, but the distinction between foot and mounted soldiers remains.

A horse gave its rider speed and impetus

Heavy machine-gun protects troops from attack

Pakistani armored personnel carrier

Armor protects crew from small-arms fire

MODERN WARFARE

The modern soldier no longer walks or marches to the battlefield or scene of engagement but is taken there in an armored personnel carrier (APC) or perhaps even flown in by helicopter. Once in action, he is armed with the latest hi-tech weaponry and is protected by tanks and other short- and long-range artillery. A soldier's life is precious and every effort is made to protect him on and off the battlefield.

Caterpillar tracks help APC to maneuver on rough ground

WHO IS IN CHARGE?

An army owes its ultimate loyalty to the head of state, such as the president or king. In practice, the head of state is usually only the honorary head of the army, which is controlled by the government. The army sometimes takes control of the country itself, as has happened in Burma, where the head of the army, General Than Shwe (right), is also head of state.

NON-MILITARY TASKS

Soldiers are often called upon to carry out non-military tasks. These Chinese soldiers are preparing to dig out survivors from the rubble after an earthquake decimated Sichuan province in 2008. Their fitness, discipline, and readiness for action make the armed forces ideal for helping civilians caught up in natural disasters and other emergencies.

Joining up

EVERY ARMY NEEDS young recruits to replace those killed or injured in combat and older men who are retiring from active service. Now recruits enlist, or join up, in two ways: either as volunteers or as conscripts. Volunteering is the preferred option, since the recruits want to join the armed services and are willing to fight. Sometimes, however, particularly during wartime, the number of recruits is too low for the army's needs, and so young men are drafted, or forced to serve. This is done by compiling a list of all young men across the country who are fit and able, and then picking groups to fight, choosing them either by age or by the day on which they were born.

THE DRAFT
When World War II broke out in Europe in 1939, the US remained neutral at first. It did, however, register men between the ages of 21 and 36, and conscript, or draft, some of them to serve in the army. Among those drafted were these men from New York, who were assigned to the US Army Air Corps. This was the first time the Corps had opened up its ranks to black recruits.

British World War I recruiting poster

PROPAGANDA
One of the most effective ways to encourage young men to join the army is through a large-scale propaganda campaign. At the outbreak of World War I in 1914, the British used the well-known face of Lord Kitchener—a famous war hero—to persuade young men to enlist. Three years later, when the US entered the war, the figure of Uncle Sam—a symbol of the US—was used for the same purpose.

World War I US recruiting poster

Army logo is prominently displayed on hood and sides of car

ATTRACTING ATTENTION
Today's armed services have come up with novel ways to attract possible recruits. The US Army sponsors a car and driver in the NASCAR stock car racing championship and takes an interactive recruiting exhibition to most races, attracting up to 1,200 potential recruits to the 1 million-strong army at each event. The exhibition also travels to hot rod races and rodeos. In addition, recruiting officers visit schools and set up stands in shopping malls.

THE KING'S SHILLING
During the 18th and 19th centuries, the daily pay in the British army or navy was 1/- (one shilling). Men who agreed to serve in the forces were said to "take the king's (or queen's) shilling." Recruiting officers used tricks to enlist young men, such as dropping a shilling into a pint of beer. By drinking the beer, the unwilling recruit had accepted the shilling and was now in the forces.

8

NATIONAL SERVICE
Some countries maintain conscription in order to keep their armed forces up to strength. These Russian men, for example, are some of those aged between 18 and 27 required by law to undertake one year's national service. Such service is also compulsory in Germany, Israel, and Switzerland. Most countries, however, have moved away from national service toward a totally volunteer army.

Ceremonial
Landsknecht
broadsword

*Extra-wide
quillons
to protect
hands*

Landsknecht
pike

MERCENARIES IN HISTORY
Most men fight for their country, but some fight just for money. Known as mercenaries, they serve whichever side will pay them. Mercenaries flourished when national rulers could not raise enough troops from home. The Landsknechts from Germany fought for various European rulers in the 15th and 16th centuries and were renowned for their brutality on and off the battlefield.

Landsknecht
halberd

*Steel ax
head*

*Uniform distinguishes a
contractor from a regular
army member*

*Long wooden
shaft*

*Steel frame
protects shaft*

MODERN MERCENARIES
Today's mercenaries, often called "private security contractors," work for private companies. These mercenaries work in Afghanistan as security guards. The largest number of private contractors—some 30,000—are found in Iraq, forming the second-largest occupation force there after US regular troops.

RESERVE FORCES
Most countries maintain a reserve force that can be called upon in times of emergency. The 350,000-strong Army National Guard, formed in 1903 out of various state forces, is the reserve force for the US army. Its motto, "Always ready, always there," sums up its role. Britain's Territorial Army, formed in 1908, performs a similar function.

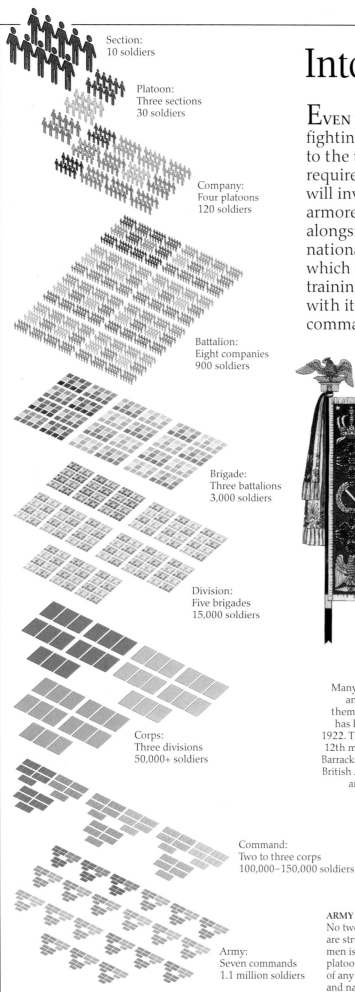

Section:
10 soldiers

Platoon:
Three sections
30 soldiers

Company:
Four platoons
120 soldiers

Battalion:
Eight companies
900 soldiers

Brigade:
Three battalions
3,000 soldiers

Division:
Five brigades
15,000 soldiers

Corps:
Three divisions
50,000+ soldiers

Command:
Two to three corps
100,000–150,000 soldiers

Army:
Seven commands
1.1 million soldiers

Into the army

Even the largest armies consist of small groups of fighting men that combine in different ways according to the task in hand. A major military expedition will require an entire army corps, while simple guard duty will involve no more than a single section. Specialized armored, artillery, and engineering units operate alongside regular infantry units in this structure. Some national armies also maintain a regimental structure, in which each regiment is responsible for recruiting and training soldiers. It is often a historic organization, with its own traditions and local connections, and commands great loyalty from its members.

French imperial eagle on a
standard of Emperor Napoleon

COLORS AND STANDARDS
Although used today only for ceremonial purposes, colors and standards (flags) once had immense importance to soldiers. They helped them to recognize their unit and rally to it in the confusion of battle. Emperor Napoleon I adopted the eagle—the symbol used by ancient Romans— as France's national symbol, and all regiments carried one into battle.

THE MASCOT
Many army units have their own mascot, an animal or object thought to bring them good luck. The US Marine Corps has had a bulldog as its mascot since 1922. The current dog, Chesty, is their 12th mascot and lives in the Marine Barracks at Washington, D.C. In the British Army, wolfhounds, goats, and rams, among others, all serve as mascots to a regiment.

US Marine
Corps bulldog
mascot

ARMY STRUCTURE
No two armies have exactly the same size or structure, but most armies are structured much like the Indian army (left). A section of ten or so men is the smallest fighting group. Sections are then organized into platoons, companies, and battalions, which are the main fighting units of any army. Above this level are brigades, divisions, corps, and regional and national commands. Together, they all make up a modern army.

Cap badge is usually positioned over left eye

Side view of a British army
Glengarry cap

Capercaillie feathers decorate this combat helmet

Soldier from Italian
Bersaglieri corps

IDENTIFYING BADGES
It is often fairly difficult to tell which army unit a soldier is from. All soldiers wear the same battle uniform when not on ceremonial parade. One way is to check the badge sewn on to his cap or to the sleeve of his uniform, since each unit has a different badge.

The Hat Terrai Gurkha is a piece of ceremonial headgear worn on parades

REGIONAL UNITS
Soldiers from a particular region are often grouped together in regiments, if they share the same background and local language as their comrades. The Gurkhas of Nepal fight in both the British and Indian armies and are renowned for their bravery and strength.

HEADGEAR
Some regiments wear distinctive headgear to identify themselves. The Italian *Bersaglieri* ("sharpshooters") wear a ceremonial wide-brimmed hat decorated with capercaillie (wood grouse) feathers, and sometimes even add the feathers on their combat helmets.

Combat medals

Distinctive red and green epaulettes

White peaked kepi

Belt buckle with badge

WEAR IT WITH PRIDE
A military uniform is not only a practical form of clothing, but also an expression of pride. The French Foreign Legion has a seven-point code of honor, which includes taking pride in wearing the uniform of a legionnaire with its distinctive white *kepi* hat.

First days

THE FIRST DAYS of being a soldier are just like the first days at a new school. There is a new building—the barracks—to find your way around, new rules and regulations to learn and obey, a new daily timetable to get used to, and a vast amount of information to absorb and use. The biggest difference from life as a civilian is that a soldier is no longer free to come and go as he pleases. His life is now totally controlled by the army, and almost every minute of the day is filled with education, training exercises, and a tough regime of physical fitness. There is little time to relax, and even less time to enjoy oneself.

Hair clippers

APPEARANCE
New recruits are given a military haircut—short back and sides—and instructed to remove all jewelry except a wedding ring if married. They are given a basic uniform and told to keep this clean and neat at all times. By now a recruit has lost his old identity and begun to take on the appearance of a young soldier.

BARRACKS
Every new soldier is assigned to a barracks or military camp. This will be his home while he is being trained. The barracks contains accommodation, a parade ground for drill (see pp.14–15), and a wide range of training, physical exercise, and sports facilities. The barracks is well guarded, and access to it is strictly controlled for security reasons.

Army food is basic but nutritional

ARMY MESS
Once in the barracks, soldiers are expected to eat, sleep, and train together. The army mess or cafeteria, such as this one used by US soldiers in Baghdad, is a good place to get to know your fellow soldiers, as well as to obtain regular meals and refreshments throughout the day.

5-gallon (23-liter) water carrier aids fitness

KEEPING FIT
Physical fitness is stressed from a recruit's very first day. The British Army, for example, puts recruits through a three-stage fitness program that at the final stage requires them to do 65 sit-ups in three minutes; six "heaves," or pull-ups (hanging from a beam and pulling your body up until your chin is clear of the top); and a 1.5-mile (2.4-km) run to be completed within 10 minutes and 30 seconds.

Afghan recruits in training

Handcuffs

CODES OF CONDUCT
Soldiers in every army have to obey military codes of conduct and laws. Punishment varies from a verbal rebuke to a reduction in rank. In extreme cases, an offender is tried by Court Martial, the court that tries those subject to military law, and may be imprisoned or even, in some countries, executed.

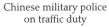

Chinese military police on traffic duty

MILITARY POLICE
Soldiers are typical of the community they come from and are just as likely to break the law as a civilian. The role of the military police, such as these Chinese officers, is to investigate soldiers' breaches of civilian criminal law and military law, arresting and charging offenders and bringing them before military justice.

RELIGIOUS GUIDANCE
The army chaplain is an ordained minister who serves in the army but does not carry weapons. His role is to provide spiritual and moral guidance to servicemen and their families, regardless of religion or belief, and to hold religious services.

Drill

A SOLDIER MUST LEARN discipline and total obedience in order to fight. Indiscipline or disobedience could endanger his life and those of the men around him. This discipline is taught through drill, the repetitive carrying out of orders so that they become second nature. Drill is taught mainly on the parade ground, where soldiers march in strict formation under the watchful eye and loud voice of their commanding officer. Square-bashing, as this is called, teaches soldiers how to obey commands. Drill also forms the basis of all military ceremonies and formal state occasions, such as the visit of a foreign head of state, when ranks of soldiers parade in colorful formation. Last, but not least, drill also teaches a soldier to take pride in his uniform.

THE TORTOISE
Roman soldiers drilled extensively to prepare them for combat. They used the *testudo*, or tortoise formation, to attack the walls or gate of a city, holding their shields to protect them from above and from all sides. This enabled them to move right up to the city with less risk of injury from enemy arrows or other missiles.

BASIC DRILL
The most basic drill every soldier learns is how to salute another soldier, particularly an officer. A salute shows respect and trust and is the normal greeting between soldiers of whatever rank. Failure to return a salute shows a lack of discipline and courtesy.

Eyes straight ahead, chin up, shoulders back

Sri Lankan soldiers on parade

Commanding officer leads his company from the front

Every soldier marches in step

ON PARADE
Every soldier learns how to march in step on a parade ground. This might seem like a pointless exercise, since it appears to have little to do with fighting an enemy, but it teaches soldiers discipline and precision. The ability to obey instantly a command barked out on a parade ground by a commanding officer could well save your life and those of your comrades if that command were issued in battle.

Drill blocks showing a battalion of six companies drawn up in two ranks

Front rank of company

Color party (regimental colors and escort)

Markers and guides help soldiers keep in straight lines

Rear rank of company

Lieutenant colonel

Junior major commands left wing of battalion

Adjutant (commanding officer's personal staff officer)

Sergeant major shouts commands

Captain of rear rank

Captain of front rank

Senior major commands right wing of battalion

DRILL BLOCKS

During the 18th and 19th centuries, officers learned to drill large bodies of men so that they could move companies (about 100 men) and battalions (800 men) from a marching column up to the line of battle without getting them "clubbed," or tangled up. They learned this skill through the use of drill blocks, each one of which represented an individual or group of soldiers.

Cotton undershirt has wide sleeves

CEREMONIAL UNIFORM

Soldiers have a dress uniform that they wear on ceremonial parades, where they may perform special drills. The outfits of the Greek *evzones* (presidential guards) have evolved from those worn by the *klephts* (mountain warriors), who fought the Ottoman Turkish rulers of Greece until independence was won in 1829.

Foot raised high in ceremonial marching step

KEEPING UP APPEARANCES

Keeping boots highly polished and a uniform clean and well pressed teaches a soldier the importance of attention to detail. As with drill, an emphasis on neatness and cleanliness creates the discipline that makes a soldier obey orders without question. A sharp uniform also gives a soldier pride in his appearance and confidence in himself and his unit.

Fustanella, a kiltlike garment

Brass bar for adjusting size of pace

Pace-stick

THE THIN RED LINE

Hours spent on the parade ground came in handy when soldiers were required to march in line toward an enemy. British redcoats—as British soldiers were once known—advanced side by side in strict formation so that they could use their muskets and bayonets effectively. These Scots Fusilier Guards advanced against the Russians in 1854 at the Battle of Alma during the Crimean War.

MEASURING THE PACE

Soldiers are trained to take paces of the same length, with the same number each minute, so that they all move at the same speed across a parade ground and do not bump into one another. The British Army still uses this pace-stick—in effect, life-size dividers—to measure the length of these paces.

Training

ALONGSIDE DRILL, a recruit undergoes training in the handling and use of weapons. This includes how to strip down and rebuild a rifle, how to fire it accurately at a target, and how to use a rifle while on the move. He learns essential skills such as radio communications and map reading, and goes on orienteering exercises to put those skills into practice. A recruit also undergoes a course of adventure training, surviving in often wild terrain by camping out and cooking his own food. These and other skills are then put to the ultimate test on full-scale maneuvers designed to simulate a real battle.

Rifle barrel is cleaned with a lightly oiled cloth

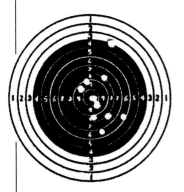

TARGET PRACTICE
Learning how to adjust the sight of your rifle so that your target is in view, and then firing accurately at the center of that target, is an essential skill. In combat, that target could be an enemy soldier aiming a rifle at you, and you may only have one chance to get it right.

Weapon parts laid out on clean, dry surface

RIFLE DRILL
When rifles were equipped with bayonets—blades that stuck out in front of the muzzle (front of the rifle)—recruits had to learn how to use this stabbing weapon in close combat. These British trainee Royal Marines from 1942 are practicing lunging at sandbags.

KNOW YOUR WEAPON
Every soldier must learn how to strip down and clean his rifle so that it remains in good working condition. A dirty rifle that has not been properly maintained might misfire or not fire at all, putting the soldier's life at risk. There is a proper order to dismantling and reassembling a rifle that does not damage it, but will reveal any wear and tear and enable a new part to be installed.

Cut at head   St. George

St. George   Cut at head

Rifle is pointed down to prevent an accident

Feint at leg   Shift

FIRE AND MANEUVER
Once the essential training of handling and firing a weapon indoors against a static target has been learned, it is time to apply those skills when moving around in the open air. These Israeli soldiers have learned how to advance toward an enemy when holding a rifle, crouching down at times to take cover or to aim at a target.

St. George   Cut at head

MAP READING
Soldiers learn how to read and understand a map and its many signs and symbols. They learn how to figure out the direction they are facing using a compass or by observation, and then how to find their position on the map. Such skills are essential when trying to find your way in foreign or dangerous territory.

Cut at leg   Shift

Maps of Normandy for World War II D-Day landings

German Leopard 1 battle tanks during maneuvers in Norway

St. George   Cut at head

COMBINED MILITARY EXERCISES
All a soldier's training comes into use when he is sent on a full-scale military exercise. Regiments work together as they would in combat and every effort is made to simulate, or mock up, a full-scale military engagement. Exercises often take place abroad, in snowy, desert, or jungle conditions not available at home.

Cut at ribs   Outside half hanger

TRAINING IN THE PAST
When soldiers carried swords as weapons, they would practice swordfighting for many hours. These illustrations, from an early 19th-century British drill book, show some of the many attacking and defending positions a soldier needed to know. Such skills survive today in the sport of fencing.

Private PV2

Private First Class

Corporal

Sergeant

Staff Sergeant

Sergeant First Class

Master Sergeant

First Sergeant

Sergeant Major

Command
Sergeant Major

Sergeant Major
of the Army

LOWER RANKS IN THE US ARMY
The lowest rank in the US army is a Private PV1, who wears no insignia on his uniform. After a few months' service, he may advance to PV2, and then to Private First Class. If he is promoted to a corporal, he becomes an NCO (non-commissioned officer) and commands a section. NCOs can be promoted to become commissioned officers.

OFFICER TRAINING
Future officers enter special military academies such as West Point in the US, École Spéciale Militaire de Saint-Cyr in France, and Sandhurst in the UK. Here they are trained in the skills they will need to command large numbers of troops. These academies are like military universities. The standards are high and students are required to learn technical and managerial as well as military subjects.

Rising through the ranks

AN ARMY OFFICER HAS A RESPONSIBILITY to look after his men and to lead them in whatever military task he is ordered to undertake. The higher the rank he holds, the more men he commands and the more responsibilities he has. Most officers enter the army as trainees and attend special military academies, although some are promoted from being ordinary privates. Officers wear badges called insignia to mark them out as men of authority whose commands must be obeyed.

Second Lieutenant

First Lieutenant

Captain

Major

Lieutenant Colonel

Colonel

Brigadier General

Major General

Lieutenant General

General

General of the Army

US COMMISSIONED OFFICERS' BADGES
A commissioned officer is a soldier who has been given a commission to hold authority within the army. In the US army, junior commissioned officers—Lieutenant and then Captain—command platoons and companies. Senior or field officers—Major up to Colonel—command battalions. Generals—who are awarded stars—command brigades and divisions.

French officer cadets at École Spéciale Militaire de Saint-Cyr

PROMOTION

Officers are promoted to the next rank according to their abilities and experience. Most promotions take place during ceremonial parades at barracks. But occasionally an officer is promoted in the field to replace an injured comrade or as a mark of instant recognition of their bravery or leadership qualities.

OFFICER'S SWORD

The sword was once the main fighting weapon of an infantry soldier but gradually lost its role in combat as muskets and then rifles took over after the 16th century. Swords are now worn only as part of an officer's full dress or ceremonial uniform at military parades, official receptions, and other special occasions.

Scabbard

Belt to hold sword

Civil War Union officer's dress sword

Ceremonial sash

Belt supported by strap worn diagonally over right shoulder

SAM BROWNE BELT

The Sam Browne is a wide leather belt designed originally to carry a sword, a weapon worn only by officers. Today, its main function is to carry a pistol. It is mainly worn by senior military and police officers. The belt gets its name from an officer with the British Army in India who lost his arm fighting in 1858 and found the belt helped him to continue wearing a sword.

US artillery officer from World War I

Roman centurion's helmet

THE CENTURION'S CREST

Army officers traditionally wore a brightly colored headpiece so that their men could see them and follow their commands in battle. Roman centurions in charge of a century (unit) of about 80 men wore a crest or plume of colored horsehair on their helmets. During the Roman Republic (509–27 BCE), a centurion's crest ran along his helmet from front to back. Soon after the Roman Empire was established in 27 BCE, its direction was changed so that it ran from side to side.

Fringe of gold braid bullions

EPAULETTES

An epaulette (a French word meaning "little shoulder") is an ornamental piece of braid that is worn on the shoulder of an officer's uniform. Epaulettes indicate the rank and regiment of the officer. Officers once wore epaulettes into battle but their visibility made them vulnerable to enemy marksmen. They are now worn only on ceremonial occasions.

Signals and intelligence

GOOD COMMUNICATIONS and intelligence (information) are as important to the modern soldier as reliable weapons and a supply of ammunition. A soldier needs to keep in regular contact with his fellow soldiers and with his base in order to receive orders and signals and pass on important information. He also needs good intelligence about the enemy: their location, strength, capabilities, and intentions. Without such intelligence, he would be operating blind and could put the lives of himself and others at risk.

MILITARY RUNNERS
Before telephones and radios, messages had to be passed by hand or word of mouth. Paul Revere rode through the night of April 18–19, 1775, warning that the British were about to seize military stores in Concord, Massachusetts. The first shots of the Revolutionary War were fired the next day.

IN COMMUNICATION
Out on operations, soldiers communicate with each other and with their base using a VHF (very high-frequency) transceiver, a radio that transmits and receives. These radios are small and light enough to be carried in a backpack. They are powered by battery and are effective over a range of up to a few miles, although some also use satellite technology to communicate farther afield or in mountainous terrain.

POSTAL PIGEON
Carrier pigeons make ideal mail carriers since they have a homing instinct that helps them return to base. The pigeons are taken far from base and may be dropped by parachute. Messages are then tied in tiny canisters to their legs, and the birds fly back to base. Carrier pigeons played a vital role in both world wars. For example, they carried Allied messages before the D-Day invasion of France in June 1944, since radios could not be used for fear of enemy interception.

Postal pigeon dropped by parachute

Satellite phone handset

Fold-out satellite dish

Cord connecting handset to satellite phone

Vest stops bird from flying home until message is attached

Backpack contains communication equipment

OVER THE DIN OF BATTLE

The sounds of rifle, cannon, and artillery fire turn battlefields into extremely noisy places and disrupt communications between an officer and his men. One way around this problem was to use loud musical instruments—a burst of notes on a bugle, or a roll of drums— to convey orders and signals to the troops over the noise of battle.

Copper and brass bell broadcasts sound over long distances

Military bugle

Balloon high in sky to avoid enemy gunfire

Cord for hanging the bugle over the shoulder when not in use

Wings can be adapted to carry up to four missiles

Pusher propeller

Synthetic Aperture Radar (SAR) spots moving targets

Warrior UAV

U.S. ARMY
WARRIOR

AERONAUTICAL SYSTEMS

Multispectral targeting system (MTS) contains infrared sensors and laser rangefinder

EYES UP ABOVE

Before the days of airplanes, military observers could watch enemy troop movements from passenger balloons or even kites. In 1794, French observers on board the reconnaissance balloon *l'Entreprenant* passed on information about Austrian troop movements in the Battle of Fleurus to their commander, Jean-Baptiste Jourdan, helping him achieve a notable victory.

AERIAL RECONNAISSANCE

The gathering of information on the enemy is known as reconnaissance. This may be done by land or by air. Increasing use is now being made of UAVs (unmanned aerial vehicles), which fly over enemy territory and send back photos and other data. UAVs vary in size from handheld models to aircraft the size of a small plane. They are controlled by radio and can largely avoid detection by enemy radar.

FOOT PATROL

The best intelligence about enemy troop positions is often obtained on foot. Reconnaissance patrols regularly go out in a combat zone—at great risk to their own lives—to obtain information at close quarters, sometimes observing the enemy for days at a time using powerful binoculars.

Antireflection lenses prevent glare from revealing their user's position

The engineers

MILITARY ENGINEERS are an essential part of an army and help it to move, fight, and live. They provide an army with all the technical support it needs to engage the enemy, including expertise in communications, construction, and weapons. These highly trained specialists build bridges, roads, and railroads, construct forts, dig defensive trenches, and erect temporary barracks, mess halls, and medical field centers. They are particularly skilled at handling explosives and at defusing or destroying unexploded bombs and mines. In the past, engineers built castles and fortifications and helped soldiers attack and capture enemy castles and walled towns. Some engineers became so skilled at building forts that they are still remembered today as great architects.

Siege tower

LAYING SIEGE
In Europe during the Middle Ages, engineers built siege towers, which soldiers used to climb the walls of a city they were besieging. Engineers also dug tunnels under the walls, which they supported with wooden props. The props were then set on fire to bring the walls tumbling down.

"Wheelbarrow" radio-controlled robot

Camera mounted on front of movable arm

Pigstick waterjet disruptor fires water into a bomb to disrupt its electronic circuits

Movable arm

Camera mounted on rear of movable arm

Screen shows pictures broadcast by robot

BOMB DISPOSAL
One of the most dangerous tasks military engineers undertake is disposing of unexploded bombs. Some of these bombs may have been left as booby traps, while others just failed to explode. Bomb disposal experts used to work by hand, but can now direct robots to do the dangerous work for them. They must first identify the kind of bomb they are faced with, using X-rays to see inside the firing mechanism. They can then decide how best to make it safe.

Large wheels to cover rough terrain

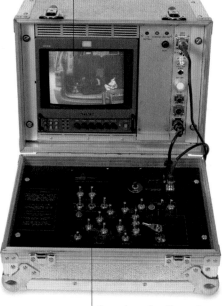

Control panel to direct robot and adjust camera angles

BLOW UP
Army engineers are often required to set up a controlled explosion to detonate stockpiles of weapons and ammunition. Iraqi National Guardsmen did this with eight tons of former Iraqi Army munitions outside Basra in 2004. Such explosions must be carefully planned to minimize risk to the engineers and any noncombatants in the area.

Landmine detector from World War II

Control handle

CLEARING A WAR ZONE
Millions of landmines lie undiscovered in the ground in current and former war zones such as Afghanistan and Bosnia. They can kill or maim their victims and render the land too dangerous for agriculture until they have all been destroyed. Trained engineers locate and detonate the mines, but the cost is considerable—at up to $2 million for each square kilometer (0.4 square miles).

Detector plate locates the metal landmine using electromagnetism

Pressure-sensitive pad triggers explosion

Antitank mine

Barracks and arsenal at center of fort surrounded by high walls

Central parade ground

Inner walls higher than outer walls to give defenders clear views outside fort

FORTIFICATIONS
By the mid-1600s, most existing fortifications were rendered useless by high-powered artillery fire. The chief military engineer of French king Louis XIV was Sébastien de Vauban (1633–1707). He solved the problem by building star-shaped forts that gave defenders excellent lines of fire and left no blind spots for attackers to exploit. He built more than 30 new forts, improved the fortifications of about 300 cities, and conducted more than 50 sieges of enemy fortifications.

Heavily fortified entrance

Model of a typical Vauban fortress

Cannon balls glance off the angled walls

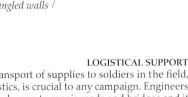

LOGISTICAL SUPPORT
The reliable transport of supplies to soldiers in the field, known as logistics, is crucial to any campaign. Engineers are often called upon to repair roads and bridges and if necessary construct new ones to replace those bombed or destroyed in war. Here, engineers of the US 2nd Infantry Division's 50th Engineer Company are constructing a floating bridge during a training exercise in South Korea.

Battle dress

THE UNIFORM WORN BY SOLDIERS on a battlefield has always depended on the types of weapon being used. Up to the 15th century, soldiers wore body armor against arrows, spears, pikes, and swords. But armor could not provide protection against muskets. These firearms, along with cannons, filled the battlefield with smoke. So soldiers started to wear colored uniforms that distinguished them from their enemy. Since the development of smokeless explosives in the 19th century, soldiers have worn brown, green, and khaki (dust-coloured) uniforms.

ARMOR
Right from the time of the ancient Greeks, soldiers wore armor made of linked sheets of metal to protect themselves against arrows, spears, and swords. Armor, such as the Roman body armor above, was effective, but was also hot and heavy to wear and restricted a soldier's ability to move.

IDENTIFICATION
The firearms and artillery used in battle after the 15th century used gunpowder as their explosive, producing dense clouds of smoke as soon as they were fired. Within minutes, the battlefield became totally obscured and soldiers were in great danger of being shot by their own side. Distinctive uniforms in national colors were adopted. The British infantry started wearing red in 1645. Different colored collars, cuffs, and other details showed the soldier's regiment and rank.

Red stands out in the smoke of battle

Yellow buttons show the officer belongs to the 44th regiment

White breeches

British officer from the Revolutionary War

Helmet moulded from Kevlar

Kevlar breastplate protects the torso

Flap of Kevlar armor protects the groin

Camouflaged uniform of brown, green, and khaki

BODY ARMOR
The modern soldier goes into battle wearing protective body armor, much as his predecessor did 500 and more years ago. This armor is made of Kevlar, a synthetic fiber that is five times stronger than the same weight of steel. It protects a soldier's torso and groin against bullets and small fragments of exploded metal, known as shrapnel.

Modern soldier wearing body armor

SHAPE SHIFTERS
Soldiers wear patterned clothing known as camouflage to hide them from the enemy. Camouflage breaks up the shape of the soldier, which helps to keep him hidden while advancing through undergrowth or greenery. The Israeli army provides its soldiers with a *mitznefet* ("clown") helmet cover that disguises the shape of the soldier's head.

Stick bound to back of shield by two rows of hide strips

Pattern indicating warrior's regiment and status

Shield made from stiffened and treated cowhide

Zulu warrior's shield

FACE PAINT
Soldiers undertaking particularly dangerous missions that require them to remain as hidden as possible apply camouflage paints to cover their exposed faces. These paints are applied like makeup, come in a range of colors, and can easily be washed off with soap and water.

CONFUSING THE ENEMY
Every army tries to trick its opponents into thinking it is stronger than it really is. Zulu warriors in southern Africa carried their shields to one side to make it appear that a man was standing next to them and fool the enemy into thinking their army was twice its real size.

HIDING AT NIGHT
Ninja warriors skilled in espionage, sabotage, assassination, and all the martial arts first emerged in Japan during the 15th century. They wore black uniforms if they were attacking at night, white uniforms if they were fighting in the snow, or the clothing of a Japanese peasant if they were in disguise.

Jika-tabi *(boots) have a split-toe design to improve grip and aid wall climbing*

Winter camouflage

Grays and white imitate snowy conditions

Jungle camouflage

Colors and shapes imitate jungle foliage

MODERN CAMOUFLAGE
Depending on whether they are fighting in the jungle, in winter conditions, or in the desert, soldiers wear differently patterned camouflage that closely matches the natural surroundings. The camouflage protects troops fighting at close quarters from sniper fire. It also protects those who are advancing toward an enemy for a surprise attack.

"Chocolate chip" desert camouflage

Weaponry

MODERN SOLDIERS MAY CARRY one or more out of many different handheld weapons into combat. They use assault rifles in attacks, or light machine guns to provide covering fire to support attacking troops. Light mortars lay down supportive shellfire to distract and disrupt the enemy, although grenade launchers can replace them. Soldiers carry pistols and hand-thrown grenades for close combat. They are given extensive training to ensure they make the best use of all the weapons they carry.

BOW AND ARROW
The longbow was the most effective long-distance weapon of the Middle Ages. This wooden bow shot arrows about 30 in (75 cm) long. A skilled longbowman could shoot up to 12 arrows a minute over 660 ft (200 m).

Flint

Flashpan

Trigger guard to prevent accidental misfire

Stock

MUSKET
The musket was the main firearm of European armies from the 16th century until it was replaced by the rifle in the 19th century. Its firing mechanism worked by striking a flint against a steel plate to produce sparks that ignited a flashpan of gunpowder. This then set off the main charge that propelled the bullet out of the muzzle.

Wooden stock sometimes replaced with a folding stock

Hand guard

AK-47 assault rifle

MODERN ASSAULT RIFLE
Assault rifles have automatic self-loading mechanisms, which load new rounds automatically. They can fire a single shot or a burst of automatic fire. The AK-47 or Kalashnikov assault rifle was developed by Mikhail Kalashnikov for the Soviet army in 1947. It is light, simple to use, and operates under most conditions, and about 50 million have been made in total.

Detachable magazine holds 30 rounds of ammunition

Rear sight

Lightweight alloy butt stock

Napoleonic infantry sword

SWORD
This weapon was developed over 4,000 years ago and was still carried by cavalrymen as late as the end of World War I in 1918. Many military swords, such as this short sword, were general purpose "cut and thrust" weapons. Well-directed thrusts were often more lethal than cuts.

LIGHT MACHINE-GUN
A light machine-gun can generate a greater volume of continuous automatic fire than the main assault rifles carried by attacking infantry. It is usually fired from a prone position (lying down) using a bipod (two-legged) support.

Negev light machine-gun

Curved trigger guard allows a two-handed grip

Butt houses 13-round magazine

Beretta Model 92FS

PISTOL
Soldiers use self-loading pistols for close-quarters combat, such as house-to-house fighting. The pistol is also an essential weapon in policing and security operations, where officers need to hide a small weapon in their clothing.

LIGHT MORTAR
Soldiers use light mortars to fire shells in support of combat troops. The shells explode near the enemy, allowing the combat troops to advance. These US marines are using a 60 mm mortar in a desert training exercise. Light mortars consist of a tube, base, and bipod stand for support. They fire high-explosive shells at low speed over a short range with a steep trajectory (angle of flight).

Muzzle

Austrian model 1798 musket

Barrel

Barrel band secures barrel to wooden stock

Ramrod to push bullet and gunpowder into gun

Gas cylinder through which gas is channelled to reload rifle

Fore sight for aiming

Laser target designator

Cylinder holds six 40 mm grenades

Skeleton butt stock can be folded forward

Fore grip

GRENADE LAUNCHER
Rapid-fire grenade launchers have two uses. They can fire nonlethal stun grenades against rioters in urban situations, and antipersonnel grenades (grenades designed to kill) during combat. Grenade launchers can replace light mortars on the battlefield as they fire a greater weight of bombs.

Mechem/Milkor MGL Mk1 grenade launcher

Safety pin is pulled out to activate the grenade

Bipod stand folded under gas cylinder

HAND GRENADES
Antipersonnel grenades can be hurled a short distance before they explode. Fragmentation grenades throw out shrapnel to wound rather than kill. Stun grenades explode with a blinding flash and deafening noise designed to stun or incapacitate people. Smoke grenades create smoke as a signaling device for incoming troops, and incendiary grenades start fires.

Russian RGD-5 grenade

Russian F1 grenade

Artillery

HEAVY WEAPONS THAT FIRE large, high-powered explosive devices are used to attack distant targets, to hold back the enemy until ground troops have taken up their positions, and to support an army in battle. Known as artillery, these pieces use indirect fire, aiming without seeing the target through their sights. Some modern weapons are now capable of firing explosives that have their own internal guidance systems. These hit the targets much more accurately.

EARLY EXPLOSIVES

The Chinese discovered how to make gunpowder—an explosive mixture of sulfur, charcoal, and potassium nitrate—during the 9th century, and first used it in warfare in the 10th century. A rocket that fired arrows was used against the invading Mongols in 1232, although it is unclear if the arrows also had exploding heads or were simply propelled by gunpowder.

Barrow of arrows is aimed by hand

Early Chinese arrow launcher

155 mm refers to the internal caliber (width) of the gun barrel

Secure base keeps gun stable

Pivoting arm

Sling to hold stone missile

Hauling ropes attached to the arm to raise the sling

Rope to pull arm down again

TRACTION TREBUCHET

Before the 12th century, large stones were hurled using a traction trebuchet. The stone was loaded in a sling attached to one end of a wooden arm. A team of men pulled down quickly on hauling ropes attached to the other end of the arm, raising the sling at high speed. The sling then hurled the stone at the walls of the enemy castle or town.

155 mm field gun

FIELD ARTILLERY

Field artillery consists of heavy guns that provide high- or low-angle support fire to an army on the battlefield. They cannot move by themselves, and must be pulled on a carriage by powerful motor vehicles. Modern field artillery has a range, or maximum distance, of many miles, and is often fired at targets that cannot be seen by the naked eye.

US army M270 Multiple
Launch Rocket System

FIELD ROCKET SYSTEMS
Multiple launch rocket
systems (MLRS) fire coordinated
groups, known as batteries, of up to
40 rockets at targets up to 55 miles
(90 km) away. Most rocket systems fire
unguided rockets, many of which will miss their
intended target, but some modern systems can
now fire guided missiles. A computer inside the
missile receives information from satellites,
which it uses to help the missile find its target.

*M270 can launch up to
12 rockets one at a time
in under a minute*

*155 mm gun capable of
firing six rounds per minute
over 18 miles (30 km)*

SELF-PROPELLED ARTILLERY
Self-propelled artillery vehicles look like tanks but are
only lightly armored in comparison to modern battle
tanks. They are equipped with heavy field guns
capable of firing large shells or rockets and are used
on the battlefield to provide long-range, indirect
bombardment of enemy targets.

*Caterpillar tracks
provide good mobility
in all terrains*

AS90 self-propelled vehicle

HEAVY MORTAR
Mortars, like other artillery pieces,
are classified as heavy or light
according to their weight and
the caliber (internal width of
barrel). The L16 81 mm mortar
shown here might look light,
but it can fire 12 10-lb
(4.5-kg) shells per minute up
to 3½ miles (5.7 km). It is
carried to the battlefield on
a truck, but is then taken
off the truck and fired from
the ground. Its main use is
to hold back the enemy until
troops arrive at close range.

*Quadrant used
to set angle
of cannon*

*Angle from
cannon to target
measured by
second quadrant*

Target

SIEGES
Historically, an army fired artillery to
break down the walls of a city or fort
during a siege. Infantry would then
pour in through the gaps. During
the Turkish bombardment of
Constantinople in 1453, the Turks
drew up a 25-ft (8-m) long cannon
that could fire a 1,200-lb (540-kg)
cannonball more than a mile. The
cannon required 400 men and
60 oxen to pull it into position.

TRAJECTORY
Today, gunners use electronics and computers to
aim an artillery piece. In the past, gunners used a
quadrant to calculate the trajectory (angle) of fire
in order to work out how far a missile would go
and where it would fall. Maximum range was
achieved at an angle of about 45°. If it were
aimed higher or lower, the missile would often
fall short of its target.

Ready for battle

MILITARY THEORIST
The Prussian general Carl von Clausewitz (1780–1831) was one of the first modern generals to think about war as a subject to study. In his book *On War,* he spelled out the difference between short-term tactics and long-term strategy and said that war is a matter of planning, chance, and emotion. His views helped many generals prepare to face the enemy.

THE HOURS BEFORE A MAJOR BATTLE are a strange time for troops. They may have spent months or years in the army training for this moment, and should be fully prepared for what is about to hit them. Yet all they can do now is sit and wait for the order to advance. Some write letters or phone home, others read, listen to music, or catch up on sleep. They check their gear and make sure they have everything they will need for the days ahead. Their commanders tour the camps to give morale-boosting talks to the troops and issue final orders. Officers make sure these orders are passed properly down through the ranks. After all this activity, a strange calm descends across the army—soon the battle will begin.

THE LAST LETTER?
The night before a battle is often a time of rest, so soldiers use it to write home to their family and loved ones, make phone calls, or send emails. Others think about the day ahead of them, and hope and pray they will see their loved ones again.

Letter home from a soldier in the Civil War

Photograph belonging to a Civil War soldier

Illustrated envelope used in the Civil War

BOOSTING MORALE
The greatest military commanders often achieve success because their men trust and believe in their judgment. This trust is usually built up by direct contact between leader and led. General Montgomery, commander of the British Eighth Army in North Africa during World War II, spoke directly to his troops so that he could discuss his battle plans with them and assure them of their forthcoming success.

US soldiers study a battle plan in Korea in 1950

BATTLE PLANS
The battle plans of a military commander are transmitted by officers right down the ranks so that each section and platoon knows what it is doing, and when. It is crucial that every soldier understands his role, since there is too little time and often too much confusion in the heat of the battle for orders to be repeated.

PRE-BATTLE MANEUVERS
On the night before a battle, the two sides often maneuver to get the best position or gain an advantage over the other side. On Christmas night 1776, George Washington and his rebel American troops crossed the icy Delaware River under cover of darkness. They captured Trenton from the surprised British the next day.

CHECKING GEAR
Before going into combat, every soldier must check his gear carefully—his life could depend on it. He must ensure his weaponry is clean and his ammunition is in order, his rations are complete, and his communications equipment is functioning properly. The soldier above is serving with the US 101st Airborne Assault Division and is checking the contents of his battle rucksack before being deployed in Iraq.

US Navy F-18 Falcon takes off from the deck of an aircraft carrier

CLOSE COOPERATION
Most modern military operations involve close cooperation between the army and the other armed services. Air force and Navy jets operating overhead can clear the skies of enemy planes and bomb enemy positions. Communications between the different services must be established and clear orders given to avoid misunderstandings or, worse, the accidental death of troops from "friendly fire" from their own side.

Night-vision goggles

Head strap

FINAL RECONNAISSANCE
The night before a battle is a good time to conduct a final reconnaissance of enemy positions. Patrols go out under cover of darkness wearing night-vision goggles to check on the enemy's strength and location, and to see if they have prepared for the forthcoming combat. The information gained will be valuable in directing troops during the first few hours of battle the next day.

Sensitive lenses collect light in low-level light conditions

The battle

A PITCHED BATTLE is the most important and dangerous event any soldier will take part in. Everything he has ever learned in the army is preparation for this brutal event. No two battles are the same. However, the battle at Gettysburg, Pennsylvania, during the Civil War illustrates how the advantage can swing from side to side, and how large-scale fighting can take place within a very small area.

Union flag

Confederate flag

THE AMERICAN CIVIL WAR
In 1861, 11 largely agricultural, slave-owing states in the southern US broke away from the largely industrialized northern states of the Union and set up the independent Confederacy. Civil war then broke out between the two sides and raged until the final defeat of the Confederacy in 1865.

THE BATTLE OF GETTYSBURG
In the of summer 1863, Confederate general Robert E. Lee marched 75,000 men north to invade Union territory. On July 1 his troops headed toward Gettysburg looking for supplies. There they were confronted by a small Union cavalry force that was soon reinforced by the 88,000-strong Union army led by General George Meade. The fighting lasted until Union troops forced the Confederates to withdraw south to Virginia on July 5. Gettysburg was the largest battle ever fought on American soil: 7,863 troops of both sides were killed, 27,224 were injured, and 11,199 were captured or missing.

1 WEDNESDAY JULY 1, 7:30 A.M.
Confederate troops heading toward Gettysburg encounter a small Union cavalry force occupying hills to the north of the town. The cavalry fight a delaying action until the Union infantry can come to their rescue.

2 WEDNESDAY JULY 1, 2:00 P.M.
A major Confederate attack dislodges the Union cavalry, now supported by two infantry corps, who retreat south through the town to Cemetery Hill. By the end of the day, 27,000 Confederate troops and 22,000 Union troops have engaged in battle.

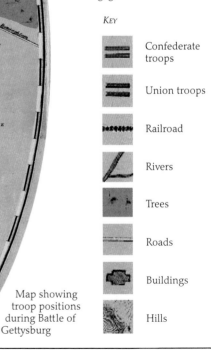

KEY

	Confederate troops
	Union troops
	Railroad
	Rivers
	Trees
	Roads
	Buildings
	Hills

Map showing troop positions during Battle of Gettysburg

3 THURSDAY JULY 2, MORNING
The rest of the Union infantry arrives south of Gettysburg throughout the morning and forms a U-shaped line along ridges and hills. Facing them to their west, north, and east, Confederate forces form a line 5 miles (8 km) long. At about 6:00 p.m. Confederate forces reach the crest of Cemetery Hill but are driven back by Union counterattacks. An hour later, the Confederates (left, in pale blue uniforms) attack Union forces (in dark blue uniforms) on Culp's Hill but fail to take it.

4 THURSDAY JULY 2, 5:00 P.M.
A major Confederate assault (from left) is launched against exposed Union lines (right) in the Wheatfield and around the Trostle Farm (above). The attack eventually reaches Plum Run Valley—the "Valley of Death"— before Union forces drive the Confederates back.

5 FRIDAY JULY 3, 4:00 A.M.
Union troops now bombard Confederate forces to drive them away from Culp's Hill. The Confederates then attack (from right) and fighting rages until 11:00 a.m. At 1:00 p.m., 150–170 Confederate guns open up their own artillery barrage against Union lines to the south on Cemetery Ridge and are answered by a Union barrage from about 80 cannon.

Confederate troops trying to climb Round Top

6 FRIDAY JULY 3, 3:00 P.M.
Both sides want to control the area surrounding Round Top to the south of the town (above). Union cavalry troops launch an attack against Confederate infantry but suffer heavy losses. A major cavalry battle also takes place 3 miles (5 km) east of the town.

7 FRIDAY JULY 3, 3:00 P.M.
After the cannon fire subsides, 12,500 Confederate troops (above), led by Major-General George Pickett, attack Union lines on Cemetery Ridge, but are repulsed. The next day, July 4, the two sides exchange limited fire. Rather than risk further casualties, Confederate forces return south on July 5.

Airborne troops

MOST SOLDIERS OPERATE SOLELY ON LAND and are transported to combat zones in armored personnel carriers and other vehicles. A select group, however, arrive at the battle by air, either dropping in by parachute, landing by glider, or arriving swiftly by helicopter or transport plane. Airborne troops have the advantages of mobility and surprise, since large numbers of these shock troops can be moved into battle at short notice and with little advance warning of their arrival. Once on land, they join up with their fellow infantry to engage with the enemy.

WAITING TO JUMP

Paratroopers are taken to the drop zone—the area above their intended landing place—in transport planes. They must be ready to jump at a moment's notice. This is where their extensive training is crucial, ensuring that they can operate under pressure. The parachute is designed to open as soon as the soldier jumps, but he can open an emergency parachute manually if the mechanism fails.

Rifle carrier

Transport plane carries paratroopers to the drop zone

Parachutes open immediately after jump

DROPPING IN

Airborne troops are useful in modern warfare since they can quickly drop in on a target that it would take ground troops a long time to reach. They can also act as advance troops for a major assault, or they can be sent in to help other forces cut off by enemy action. However, they cannot operate in poor weather and may become separated in windy conditions.

THE PARACHUTE

Parachutes are large pieces of material, about 200 sq ft (20 sq m) in size, worn wrapped up in a backpack. Once released by a ripcord, they open out to slow the descent to earth. They were once made from silk but are now made from strong, lightweight woven nylon fabric. Circular parachutes have a descent rate of 20–23 ft/sec (6–7 m/sec). Modern square designs reduce violent turns and slow the rate to a safer 16 ft/sec (5 m/sec).

French parachutist's equipment from the 1970s

Emergency parachute worn on front

Static line automatically opens the chute on leaving the aircraft

Main parachute worn on back

Shoulder harness

BEHIND ENEMY LINES

In the early hours of D-Day—June 6, 1944, when Allied troops invaded northern France during World War II—three British gliders landed by the Caen Canal in Normandy. The troops inside seized the Bénouville—later renamed the Pegasus—Bridge, a vital crossing point over the canal. This stopped the German army from sending reinforcements to fight Allied troops landing on nearby beaches. This image shows Pegasus bridge with two gliders in the background.

US Bell UH-1 Huey Helicopter in Vietnam

HELICOPTER

Helicopters have been deployed extensively in combat ever since US Marines started to use them in Vietnam during the 1960s. They can provide transport for troops, equipment, and supplies, often operating from secure bases well behind the front line or from ships anchored safely offshore.

Strap for rifle carrier

Model of a British Horsa glider used in World War II

Cockpit with pilot's compartment and door for loading freight

Glider can accommodate 28 troops or carry a jeep or a 6-pounder antitank gun

Lightweight pack for emergency provisions

GLIDING DOWN

Gliders are useful for landing troops or equipment in enemy countryside before runways and airports have been seized. Their silence is also an advantage, since they have no engines to alert enemy troops. However, the lack of power makes landings risky and a bad landing can be costly in lives and equipment.

THE FIRST TANKS
Britain developed the first tanks during World War I. They carried up to 10 men and could only be stopped by well-aimed artillery fire. The Mark V tank carried circular metal bundles that could be dropped into an enemy trench to form a bridge. Tanks like these proved decisive in the final battles of the war.

BATTLE OF KURSK, WORLD WAR II
The biggest tank battle in history took place at Kursk in western Russia in 1943. More than 2,700 German tanks attacked Soviet positions around the city but were repelled by 3,500 Soviet tanks, notably the T-34 (above). Losses were immense on both sides, but the German advance was stopped and the advantage swung to the Soviet Army.

Tank troops

EVER SINCE TANKS FIRST APPEARED during World War I (1914–18), they have made a major contribution to warfare. These armor-plated vehicles run on tracks, which means that they can cope with rough or muddy terrain. They use their vast firepower to blow up enemy defenses and smash holes in enemy lines to allow the infantry to pour in behind them. They can also fight each other in fast-moving battles. Tanks are vulnerable to antitank missiles and can't operate in mountainous or jungle terrain, but they are still one of the most important and powerful weapons on the battlefield. Tanks are typically manned by a crew of four, who have to endure the heat, noise, and cramped conditions.

Tank commander opens the turret to view surroundings

Main gun rotates through a wide angle of fire

A MODERN TANK
Today's tanks are highly mobile and heavily armed fighting machines. On most tanks, the powerful main gun is mounted on a turret. The Israeli Merkava tank shown here has a 120-mm main gun capable of firing laser-guided antitank missiles, as well as three secondary machine guns, an internal mortar, and smoke grenades.

Reinforced armor on the underside of the tank to protect it against mines

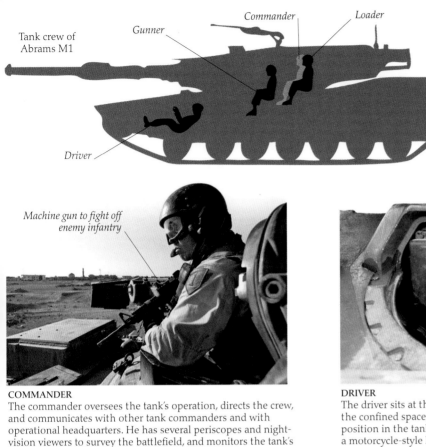

Tank crew of
Abrams M1

Gunner

Commander

Loader

Driver

THE CREW
A modern tank, such as the US Abrams M1, carries a crew of four, each with his own role. Commander, loader, and gunner work in the turret basket, the turret's interior compartment, while the driver sits in the main body of the tank. Conditions are cramped, especially for the loader who has to shift the ammunition from its storage compartment to reload the main gun and secondary weapons.

Machine gun to fight off
enemy infantry

COMMANDER
The commander oversees the tank's operation, directs the crew, and communicates with other tank commanders and with operational headquarters. He has several periscopes and night-vision viewers to survey the battlefield, and monitors the tank's operational systems on his computerized display unit.

DRIVER
The driver sits at the front of the tank under the main gun. To fit into the confined space, he lies back in a reclining chair—the most comfortable position in the tank. He navigates using three periscopes and steers with a motorcycle-style handlebar, accelerating by twisting a handle-grip throttle. He brakes using a pedal on the floor.

Turret roof is 8 ft 9 in
(2.66 m) above ground

Hull is protected by a
composite armor of ceramic,
steel, and nickel

GUNNER
The gunner controls the main gun. He pinpoints targets—such as an enemy tank or bunker—using a stabilized sight that has day vision and thermal night vision capabilities. Then he fires using a laser range-finder to measure the distance to the target. It is also the gunner's job to tell the loader what sort of ammunition to prepare and load.

TANK TACTICS
A well-positioned tank, protected by a mound or concealed by trees, can be a deadly weapon. In some cases, a tank can adopt a hull-down position, where only the turret appears above a ridge (above). From here, it can provide supporting fire for friendly troops, and take out enemy positions when they start firing and give away their location.

The marines

THE ORDER "SEND IN THE MARINES" has been issued by the US government 200 times since World War II. These soldiers are trained to be the first on the scene and ready to fight in any environment. The marines' main role is to launch rapid seaborne attacks on enemy positions on land. They arrive in amphibious vehicles, which can move in water and on land, and seize beaches and other important positions until regular soldiers can relieve them. Marines also patrol rivers and coasts and can operate on land, much as regular soldiers do. Today, nearly every country with a coastline has a marine unit as part of its armed forces.

US Marine Corps badge

LAND, SEA, AND AIR
The US Marine Corps has its origins in the 1775 Revolutionary War, when soldiers served on board naval ships. Since then, the marines have developed as a highly trained intervention force with a reputation for success. The eagle, globe, and anchor on their badge symbolize their air, land, and sea capabilities.

Assault craft can leave from rear of ship

MARINES IN COMBAT
Marines take part in combat where large, seaborne assaults on enemy positions are required. Stationed on assault ships, they come ashore in amphibious landing craft and small boats, and are prepared to fight the instant they hit the shore. This photograph of a joint Russian–Chinese training exercise held in 2005 gives a good idea of what such an assault would look like in action.

Amphibious tanks motor from ship directly to shore

Rigid raider assault craft deliver troops onto the beach

Command tower

Flight deck for helicopters

NAVAL FORCES
Japan developed two types of marines in the 19th century: special landing forces attached to the army, and sailors given infantry training. One such force fought on Ganghwa Island during the conflict with Korea in 1875 (above). Both groups were abolished at the end of World War II.

ASSAULT SHIP
Large-scale assaults are conducted from specially designed vessels, such as the French naval ship *Mistral*. Such ships have flight decks for helicopters and low-level well decks to launch small assault craft, hovercraft, and other amphibious vehicles to carry the marines ashore. The marines live on board between missions, as the ship acts as their floating headquarters and base.

HOVERCRAFT
Hovercraft are ideal vehicles for marine troops, as they can "fly" over both sea and land and cross marshy and swampy ground that other land or sea vehicles cannot navigate. The US Marines use LCAC (Landing Craft Air-Cushioned) hovercraft to transport troops, vehicles, and supplies to the shore at speeds of up to 40 knots (nautical miles per hour: 1 knot is 1.15 mph/1.85 kph).

Rubber skirt holds a layer of high-pressure air on which the hovercraft "flies"

Hatch for access and observation

RIGID RAIDER
Fast patrol and assault craft carry up to 20 marines or 1 ton of cargo at speeds of up to 30 knots laden, or 50 knots unladen. These fast craft are invaluable for rapid reconnaissance missions (gathering information), or where troops have to penetrate narrow inland rivers and waterways.

Hull made of light, glass-reinforced plastic

Single or twin 140 hp outboard motors

Tracks

AMPHIBIOUS ASSAULT VEHICLE
Amphibious landing vehicles carry marines and equipment from ships to shore and farther inland. These armored vehicles can carry up to 25 marines and are equipped with a grenade launcher and machine gun to protect them from hostile enemy fire Their caterpillar tracks grip any surface.

Special troops

THE SPECIAL FORCES are elite troops in modern conflict. Operating largely in secret and often behind enemy lines, they carry out swift and daring operations. Their main role is to fight insurgents revolting against a government, but they also rescue hostages, carry out sabotage (damage to enemy equipment), recover secret information, and protect important people. Special forces are highly trained professionals who are prepared for anything. Britain's SAS—the Special Air Service, one of the most famous special forces in operation—has the motto "Who Dares Wins." Its members risk their lives, but if they fail, the security of their country might be in danger.

Grenade launcher fires lethal, nonlethal, and illuminating rounds

9-mm rounds

15-round magazine can be exchanged for one holding 30 rounds

40-mm grenade

AIR RAIDERS
The British Special Air Services (SAS) was formed by Lieutenant David Stirling in 1941 to fly in behind enemy lines in North Africa during World War II. Initially a group of 68 volunteers, they carried out many bombing and sabotage missions, using the vast desert for cover. These men had just returned from a three-month-long mission.

WEAPONS AND EQUIPMENT
Special forces are armed with military-issue weaponry adapted for close-quarter combat work. British SAS troops carry the light but very accurate Heckler & Koch MP5 submachine gun. This has also been adapted to fire grenades, and throw stun grenades that make a bright flash and loud bang to shock their targets without causing them injury. Troops firing this weapon wear respirators worn over their balaclavas to protect against gas and smoke.

Respirator

Filter on front of respirator removes smoke particles and poisonous gases

HOSTAGE RESCUE
Special forces are skilled at surprise operations. In 1976, a Palestinian terrorist group seized an Air France airplane at Entebbe, Uganda, containing 104 Israeli and Jewish passengers. Israeli commandos from the top secret *Sayeret Matkal* unit flew to Entebbe. In a bold operation they recovered all but one of the hostages and returned them safely to Israel.

Rear sight

Retractable stock

COUNTERTERRORISM

After a Palestinian terrorist attack on Israeli athletes at the 1972 Olympic Games held in Munich, Germany, the West German government set up the GSG-9—the *Grenzschutzgruppe-9*, or "Border Guards Group 9." This was a new secret force designed to rescue hostages taken by terrorist groups operating in West Germany, and to track down the terrorists.

GSG-9 insignia

Rate-of-fire indicator can be changed between single shot, three-round burst, and automatic

MP5A5
submachine gun

IN SECRET

Special forces operate in the shadows, and the identities of individual troops are not revealed for fear of reprisals. Balaclavas cover the face while allowing the wearer to see out and shout orders and instructions. They are named after the Ukrainian town of Balaklava, where British troops wore them to keep warm during the Crimean War (1853–56). Special forces soldiers now wear them to maintain secrecy.

ELITE TRAINING

Special forces undergo rigorous training to cope with every situation. These Green Berets—the name given to the US Army special forces—are preparing to enter an abandoned building in Georgia. The building is empty, but in real life, it could contain highly armed terrorists. Special forces sometimes train in mock-up situations—a reconstruction of a real street, or an unused aircraft cabin—so that they are familiar with the terrain they are about to enter.

Camouflage netting keeps soldiers hidden as they monitor enemy movements

SURVEILLANCE

Although special forces may be involved in dangerous, fast-moving operations, much of their work is actually very dull. Every secret operation requires a vast amount of intelligence (information) gained from lengthy surveillance (careful observation). The hours and days spent watching the enemy is time well spent—when the operation starts, the forces will be prepared for every eventuality.

The medical corps

EVERY SOLDIER DREADS IT, and tries to avoid it at all costs, but one day it is likely that he will be injured in the course of duty. Up until the late 19th century, his chances of surviving a major injury were slim, since there were no antibiotics to kill infection, few effective anaesthetics to numb the pain, and surgical equipment was not sterilized before use. Today, his chances are much better. Military medicine is as good as civilian, and the army medics—surgeons, doctors, and nurses—are all professionally trained.

FLORENCE NIGHTINGALE
Florence Nightingale (1820–1910) nursed British soldiers during the Crimean War of 1853–56. She found them in a terrible condition, but soon improved their medical care. Death rates dropped dramatically. On her return to Britain, she campaigned to set up the Army Medical College, a huge step forward in the treatment of the wounded.

Canvas awning to shelter the wounded

Red Cross flag

Driver's seat

Horse-drawn ambulance

EARLY FIELD AMBULANCES
Before the development of the earliest ambulances, the wounded were left on the field until the battle was over, resulting in many deaths. The first ambulances were horse-drawn carts covered with canvas tops, like this one from the Civil War of 1861–65. Red Cross flags hung on either side and waved in front to indicate to the enemy that this was an ambulance and not a combat vehicle, so they should not fire at it. Motorized ambulances did not appear until the early years of the 20th century.

ARMORED AMBULANCE
Military ambulances are standard armored vehicles adapted to take stretchers. In accordance with the First Geneva Convention of 1864, which sets down rules for the treatment of all wounded soldiers, military ambulances must display the red cross and must not be armed. However, this does not always prevent medical teams from being fired on—accidentally or deliberately.

Chinese army medical team carry an injured civilian in Sichuan Province

Ship painted white with large red crosses to identify it as a non-combatant hospital ship

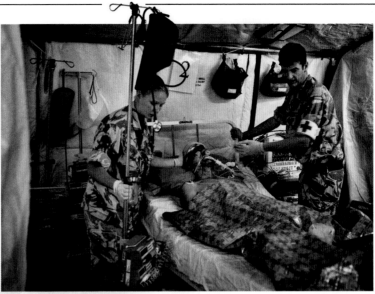

FLOATING HOSPITAL
Hospital ships contain complete operating rooms and intensive care units, as well as recovery wards. The ships can sail quickly to where they are required and can be stationed offshore or in the nearest port. Patients arrive by road or boat, or are flown in by helicopters that can land on the deck.

MOBILE MEDICAL UNIT
Today's army medics operate in a mobile field hospital equipped with the latest medical technology, including the intensive care equipment and monitors shown above. They can treat wounds—such as those caused by a grenade, as above—stop pain, and perform minor operations. Patients requiring major operations are stabilized and then—if battle conditions permit—driven by ambulance or airlifted by helicopter to the nearest hospital.

Wound dressing

Insect repellant

Iodine

Water-purifying tablets

Adhesive bandage

FIRST AID
Soldiers carry their own first aid kit in case they are injured in the field. This basic kit was issued to US Marines fighting in Vietnam in 1965–71. It included iodine to clean wounds and insect repellent. The jungle swarmed with malaria-bearing mosquitoes, and over 40,000 cases of the disease were recorded in the US Army from 1965–70.

MODERN MILITARY NURSING
Today's military nurses are highly trained professionals. They can respond quickly to any emergency and deal with patients rapidly. As a result, they are well equipped to deal with civilian disasters, such as the earthquake that devastated Sichuan province in China in 2008. Here they are taking a dehydrated survivor for treatment, while giving him fluids intravenously (directly into a vein).

K rations

D ration

Feeding the troops

THE FRENCH MILITARY GENIUS NAPOLEON BONAPARTE is alleged to have said that an army marches on its stomach. He was right, for without adequate food and water, a soldier cannot march or fight effectively, his morale weakens, and discipline breaks down in the ranks. Food is therefore as important to an army as weapons and ammunition. An army must make sure that every soldier receives enough nutritious food every day to function effectively. Mobile food kitchens follow armies around and produce vast quantities of food on demand. However, such kitchens are no use to soldiers under fire in the front line. They must carry their own food rations, preparing and eating them in the few minutes they can grab in the heat of battle.

RATIONS
During World War II, the US Army issued lightweight daily food rations to its paratroopers. K-rations consisted of a single breakfast, lunch, or supper pack of food that would not spoil, such as dry crackers, canned ham, and coffee, as well as gum and cigarettes. However, the army found that the K-ration contained too few calories to support a fighting man for long and added the D-ration—an oatmeal and chocolate energy bar.

Utensils made of lightweight alloy

Handle folds out

Mess can

Standard-issue cutlery

Wood alcohol   Hexamine   Waterproof match container

UTENSILS
Eating utensils have to be light and portable for men on the move. This knife, fork, and spoon set was issued to US paratroopers during World War II and fit into a leather pouch. Soldiers prepared their food in a mess can over a fire.

FUEL AND MATCHES
US paratroopers cooked with wood alcohol, which they poured onto wood to make it burn more easily, or with solid-fuel hexamine tablets, which burned without the need for any wood. Matches were stored in a waterproof container.

CALORIE INTAKE

The amount of energy contained in food is measured in calories. Humans need different amounts of calories according to age, gender, and occupation. Soldiers in garrison (on duty at their home base) eat up to 30 percent more calories per day than an adult civilian, but soldiers training in cold weather need almost twice as many calories.

Daily calorie requirement

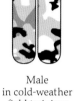

| Child aged 5–15: 1,800 calories | Adult female: 2,000 calories | Adult male: 2,500 calories | Female in garrison: 2,400 calories | Male in garrison: 3,200 calories | Female in cold-weather field training: 3,500 calories | Male in cold-weather field training: 4,500 calories |

MOBILE KITCHEN

Troops near the front line are fed from mobile field kitchens, such as this US Army kitchen, capable of producing vast quantities of warm, nourishing food for large numbers of troops at very short notice. The meals are healthy but not particularly varied, since fresh ingredients are not always available. Armies often try to cater to the different dietary needs of their soldiers—for instance, Singapore's armed forces provides three different combat rations for Muslims, non-Muslims, and vegetarians.

Villagers in Russia burned their houses when the German army invaded in 1941

SCORCHED EARTH

Traditionally, armies on the move lived off the land they moved through, scavenging food from towns, farms, and orchards, and often leaving the local population to starve after they had left. A country threatened with invasion could respond by scorching or burning the land in front of the invading army, and evacuating the local population. This drastic measure denied the invaders food and supplies, slowing or stopping their advance.

SURVIVAL FOODS

Sometimes soldiers have to find their own food. In the Outback, Australian troops are taught how to find and eat traditional Aboriginal bushfood, such as these witchetty grubs. The grubs can be eaten raw or lightly cooked. Such skills could be life-saving, since soldiers might be engaged in a long mission in remote areas or behind enemy lines where they need to be able to feed themselves.

Grub lives in the roots of the witchetty bush and is a valuable source of protein

Witchetty grubs

Morale

KEEPING IN TOUCH
Troops want to keep in touch with their families and friends back at home to reassure them they are well and safe. Modern armies provide troops with telephones and the internet, so that they can phone home and send emails. These US soldiers are phoning home from Iraq.

THE STRESS AND FEAR of fighting can undermine a soldier's ability to make the right decisions. It is therefore crucial that a soldier's morale (confidence and spirits) is kept high. Rousing speeches inspire troops about to go into battle. During quieter periods, live shows, films, music, and comedy are put on to entertain troops. They can also write home or phone friends and family, although letters are censored to prevent important information from falling into the hands of the enemy.

TROOPS ENTERTAINING TROOPS
During a war, an army often puts on its own shows, with performers drawn from its own ranks. In World War II, the British set up ENSA, the Entertainments National Service Association. It gave more than 2.5 million performances, including this one in Gibraltar in 1942.

POSTAL FLIGHT
Letters sent to and from troops serving abroad often took weeks to arrive, since they were sent by land or ship. In 1919 the world's first army postal service opened between Germany and Britain, serving British troops stationed in Germany after the end of World War I.

CENSORING MAIL

Wartime letters cannot pass unchecked through the mail in case they contain information that might help the enemy. Censors, such as these men and women in New York in 1942, regularly check all military mail and black out any offending information.

Drone produces one
sustained note

Bellows blows
air into the
chanter and
drones

Mouthpiece for
piper to blow
air into bellows

Great Highland
bagpipe

Chanter produces
the melody (tune)

INSPIRING MUSIC

Until the 18th century, Scottish soldiers fought to the sound of a massed band of pipers. The high, penetrating notes of the bagpipe could be heard above the noise of battle, inspiring the Scots to fight bravely. Today, bagpipes and other musical instruments are very rarely used in battle, but they still play a large morale-boosting role at military parades.

TV host David
Letterman
entertains US
troops in Iraq

PRE-BATTLE SPEECH

An inspiring speech before a battle can rally the troops' morale. In 1588, Queen Elizabeth I of England inspected her army as it prepared to fight the Spanish. She told them, "I know I have the body of a weak and feeble woman, but I have the heart and stomach of a king." These words did much to inspire her forces to victory.

A CONCERT

The US forces first encouraged movie stars, singers, and comedians to entertain troops serving abroad during World War II. The tradition has continued, and US troops in Korea, Vietnam, and beyond have been entertained by figures such as movie star Marilyn Monroe and comedian Bob Hope.

The end of a campaign

WHEN A WAR COMES TO AN END, those involved can be left with very mixed feelings. One side must come to terms with defeat, while the other may return home to a victory parade. Both the winners and the losers will be left to reflect on the loss of life caused by the war. Medals are awarded for bravery and outstanding soldiers are promoted, but for many troops, the end of the fighting marks an end to their army life. Thousands of soldiers may be demobilized to resume civilian life. After what could have been several years in the army, they will need help to adjust to their new lives.

Légion
d'Honneur

Victoria Cross

Medal of Honor

MEDALS OF HONOR
Most nations have a special award that is given to soldiers for outstanding bravery in battle. France awards the Légion d'Honneur (established in 1802), the US the Medal of Honor (1862), and Britain the Victoria Cross (1856).

MILITARY SPOILS
A victorious army used to return home with captured enemy banners and other trophies, including prisoners of war. They also returned with booty—money, works of art, and antiques—taken from enemy towns. This practice is less common today, although atrocities such as the rape or murder of civilians still occur.

VICTORY PARADE
A triumphant army may be offered a victory parade through the nation's capital or other major city when it returns from war, so that the people can welcome the soldiers home. Nearly five million people lined the streets of New York City in 1991 to cheer US troops returning from action in the Persian Gulf. The army had successfully liberated Kuwait from Iraqi occupation during Operation Desert Storm.

DEMOBILIZATION
Large numbers of British troops returning home after World War II were demobilized (released) from the army. These two soldiers are looking at the "demob" suits they will be given when they finally leave the army. The choice was not varied, and the quality not good, but after years in khaki, the new suit showed that the wearer was a civilian back in "civvy street."

Vietnam Service Medal   Waterloo Medal

SERVICE MEDALS
A campaign medal is awarded to soldiers who fought in a particular campaign. The Vietnam Service Medal was awarded to US military personnel who served in the Vietnam War between 1961 and 1975. The Waterloo Medal was awarded to all British soldiers of whatever rank who were present at the deciding battle against Emperor Napoleon I of France in 1815.

Red, white, and blue balloons represent the colors of the US flag

Ticker tape floats down from the buildings above

RETRAINING
Soldiers leave the army after they have completed a specified period of service or after the end of a war, when they are no longer required in such large numbers. They are offered help and retraining so that they can find a job. Most have acquired useful skills that they then use as civilians, but many find it difficult to adapt after years of following orders.

Honoring the soldier

CHELSEA PENSIONERS
Former soldiers are sometimes offered accommodation in their old age. The Chelsea Pensioners—named after the Royal Hospital in Chelsea, London, where they live—are given room, board, and a small weekly pension. They wear a ceremonial scarlet uniform and a three-cornered hat that dates back to the 18th century.

THE END OF A WAR is a time to pay respects to the soldiers—living and dead—who fought in it and in previous conflicts. The dead are honored in the memorials and cemeteries that mark where they died, and in the national monuments built to remember them at home. In many countries, a special day is set aside each year to honor those who died in past wars. In the UK, ceremonies are held on Remembrance Day, when thousands of old soldiers come together to honor their fallen comrades.

Corn poppy

Tower contains the death-bell sounded at official ceremonies

REMEMBRANCE DAY
Soldiers fighting on the Western Front during World War I took pleasure in the bright red poppies that bloomed in the soil of the battlefields. After the war ended, the poppy was adopted by ex-servicemen's groups in the UK to commemorate those who were killed. People wear paper or plastic poppies on Remembrance Day, November 11—the anniversary of the armistice (peace agreement) that ended the war in 1918.

WAR CEMETERIES
Millions of troops were killed on both sides of the Western Front during World War I. Many are buried in vast cemeteries, such as this one at Douaumont in eastern France. The cemetery contains the graves of 25,000 named soldiers, and an ossuary (a room used to store bones) holds the remains of more than 130,000 unknown soldiers. They all died fighting at the Battle of Verdun in 1916.

ANZAC DAY
Large numbers of the Australian and New Zealand Army Corps (ANZAC) fought and lost their lives in the futile Gallipoli campaign against the Turks in 1915, during World War I. Their loss, and losses during other wars, are commemorated each year on Anzac Day, April 25.

50

Sword with stainless steel blade measures 108 ft (33 m) long

ETERNAL FLAME
Throughout history, soldiers have lost their lives in war without their remains being identified. Symbolic memorials to the unknown soldier were first erected in Denmark in 1858 and the US in 1866. Such tombs are often given pride of place in the nation's capital. The Russian memorial lies next to the Kremlin Wall in Moscow. An eternal flame illuminates an inscription that says: "Your name is unknown, your deed is immortal."

Concrete figure is 170 ft (52 m) tall

The Motherland Calls statue, Volgograd, Russia

MONUMENTS TO WAR
Many countries have erected statues and other memorials to commemorate victory against the enemy. One of the most impressive is the *Motherland Calls* statue outside Volgograd in southern Russia. The city, then known as Stalingrad, was the scene of a five-month siege by German troops. The battle for the city cost over one million lives before the Germans surrendered in February 1943.

THE VIETNAM WALL
The Vietnam Veterans Memorial in Washington, D.C., lists the names of 58,256 US servicemen and women who died fighting in Vietnam between 1959 and 1975. The wall in fact consists of two separate granite walls 246 ft 9 in (75.2 m) long that meet at one end. A women's memorial and the bronze *Three Soldiers* statue stand nearby.

Plinth

RETURNING BODIES
After a battle or war has ended, the dead soldiers may be brought back for burial at home. Their coffins are often escorted by fellow soldiers and wrapped in the national flag. Here, members of the Indian Border Security Force carry back the remains of one of the 19 soldiers and 9 family members who lost their lives in 2004 during the conflict with Kashmir separatists.

Prisoners of war

Muslim soldiers with prisoners

Every soldier hopes to emerge from a battle in the company of his comrades, but sometimes he is taken prisoner by the enemy. As a POW (prisoner of war) his rights are guaranteed by the Third Geneva Convention, adopted in 1929 and revised in 1949. This international agreement governs how POWs should be treated and rules out the use of torture, among its many provisions. Warring states usually abide by it, although many POWs captured during World War II were appallingly treated. Recent disregard of the convention by Serbia and the US has attracted widespread international criticism.

THE CRUSADES
In the 11th and 12th centuries, Christians and Muslims fought for control of Palestine in the Middle East. The Christians killed many of their Muslim prisoners. The Muslims, however, treated Christian prisoners well, because Muhammad had instructed that Muslims provide for all prisoners regardless of religion.

Eyeglasses made by POWS of the Japanese during World War II

COLDITZ
Allied officers who tried to escape from German prisoner of war camps during World War II were sent to Colditz Castle as punishment. The castle was meant to be secure, but its inmates tried every method to get out. Of the 1,500 prisoners held in Colditz, 176 attempted to escape, but only 31 succeeded.

HARSH TREATMENT
During World War II, the Japanese treated their POWs with great cruelty. Thousands were forced to build railroad lines through the Burmese jungle or work in labor camps. Rations were small and new clothes nonexistent. Prisoners wore shoes until they fell apart and even made their own combs and eyeglasses.

POW comb

Miniature saw blade

ESCAPE
POWs often try to escape from captivity and make simple tools from bedposts and scraps of metal to do it. Prisoners in Colditz built a glider in the attic of the castle, but the war ended before they could use it to fly to freedom. Two Dutch officers escaped from Colditz by hiding in a manhole. Their comrades fooled the guards into thinking they were still in the camp by holding up dummies during prisoner counts.

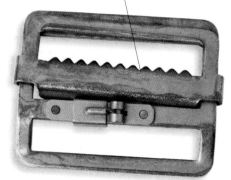

Belt buckle with hidden saw blade

Handmade saw to cut wood

MODERN TREATMENT
Although the Geneva Convention dictates how POWs should be looked after, atrocities still occur. In 1992, during the Bosnian civil war, the Serb army kept its Bosnian and Croat prisoners at Manjaca camp. The guards tortured the prisoners; at least 85 were killed and 1,000 people are still unaccounted for.

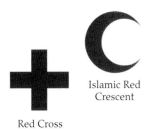

Red Cross

Islamic Red Crescent

Red Crystal sometimes used in place of the Red Cross or Red Crescent

Iranian Red Lion with Sun

Israeli Red Star of David

AID AGENCIES
The Geneva Convention allows POWs to receive letters, gifts, books, and food packages from home. The International Red Cross and Red Crescent Movement, an international humanitarian movement with an estimated 97 million volunteers, and similar smaller organizations, organize these packages. They also visit camps and check up on the health and welfare of prisoners.

PRISONER EXCHANGE
POWs are sometimes used as bargaining chips in a peace deal between two warring nations. One side offers to release the prisoners it holds in return for the release of its own nationals held by the other side. Such an exchange took place between United Nations troops and North Korea at the end of the Korean War in 1953.

Prisoners are bound and gagged to prevent movement and communication

GUANTÁNAMO BAY
Suspects captured by the US in its war against terror in Afghanistan and elsewhere since 2001 have been taken to the Guantánamo Bay Detention Camp at the US naval base in Cuba. The US government has been heavily criticized for mistreating the prisoners, including using torture to gain confessions. Until 2006, however, it refused to accept that the Geneva Conventions applied to the prisoners it held there.

Guerrilla fighters

Most soldiers fight for their country in official, national armies. Some, however, fight in unofficial groups for a specific cause, such as freeing their country from foreign occupation. Roughing it in the countryside or hiding in towns, they wear no uniforms and fight with whatever weapons they can lay their hands on. They avoid pitched battles with regular troops, since they are usually outnumbered or less well equipped. Instead, they launch surprise raids, ambush unsuspecting troops and vehicles with roadside bombs and booby traps, and fight in other unexpected ways. Such soldiers are known as guerrillas. They may be seen by some as freedom fighters, although their enemies may consider them terrorists.

THE "LITTLE WARRIORS"
The word "guerrilla" means "little war" in Spanish. The term first came into use in the Peninsular War of 1807–14, when Juan Martín Díez (above) led small groups of irregular Spanish fighters against the occupying French army. Díez's men disrupted the supply lines of the French, who were finally driven out of Spain in 1814.

LAWRENCE OF ARABIA
In 1916, during World War I, the people of Arabia rose in revolt against their Ottoman Turkish rulers. The British soldier T. E. Lawrence helped the Arabs carry out guerrilla raids against the Turks, blowing up targets such as the Hejaz Railroad. This tied down Turkish forces in defending the railroad rather than fighting the British army.

THE MUJAHIDEEN
The Islamic Mujahideen of Afghanistan were originally funded by the US and others to fight the Soviet troops that had invaded and occupied the country in 1979. They had great success in shooting down Soviet helicopters and planes, and eventually drove out the Soviets in 1989. However, the Mujahideen soon fell out among themselves, and the country descended into civil war.

Rocket-propelled grenade launcher carried by a Mujahideen fighter

Remains of a Humvee vehicle

SURPRISE TACTICS
Guerrilla forces use speed and mobility to carry out raids and ambushes. These surprise attacks work well against more powerful but less flexible enemies. Here a group of Iraqis opposed to the US invasion and occupation of their country in 2003 have planted a roadside bomb in Baghdad. The explosion has destroyed a US Humvee (High Mobility Multipurpose Wheeled Vehicle).

LOCAL KNOWLEDGE
Guerrillas have a huge advantage over traditional forces—they know their own area well and can hide in caves and remote places, fading into the background if threatened with attack. Al-Qaeda has used its local knowledge of the Tora Bora Mountains in Afghanistan to hide its leader, Osama Bin Laden, and other guerrillas from the American troops searching for them.

Cave in Afghanistan where Osama Bin Laden hid until 2004

Spiked plate

Poster urging Cubans to build on Che Guevara's achievements

BOOBY TRAPS
Guerrilla groups often make their own homemade weapons. Vietnamese guerrillas fighting US troops in the 1960s planted spiked plates into the ground. The plates pierced the foot of any soldier who trod on them. The Vietnamese also killed many US soldiers with grenades attached to tripwire— the grenades exploded when any part of the wire was touched.

Tripwire grenade

FIGHTING HEROES
Guerrilla leaders often achieve popular acclaim as revolutionary heroes fighting cruel and dictatorial regimes. Ernesto "Che" Guevara was born in Argentina in 1928, but played a major role in helping Fidel Castro come to power in Cuba in 1959. He tried to bring about revolution in Africa and South America but was killed fighting in Bolivia in 1967. His face is seen on posters in Cuba urging young people to follow his example.

Women in uniform

WHETHER WOMEN SHOULD enter battle continues to be a controversial issue, even though women have fought and died alongside men as long as there have been wars. Many men—and women, too—felt that females were not physically tough enough to fight, and would be too emotional under fire. That view is no longer universally held. Women are now admitted into most national armies and play a major role in all support services. Yet their role in front-line combat is often limited. Generals and politicians still believe it would be bad for army morale and public opinion to see large numbers of female soldiers killed, especially if they are the mothers of young children.

THE LEGENDARY AMAZONS
According to ancient Greek mythology, the Amazons were a nation of all-female warriors who lived somewhere along the shores of the Black Sea. They were descended from Ares, the god of war, and are often shown fighting on horseback against Greek foot soldiers.

FRANCES CLAYTON
Many women have put on men's clothes and fought alongside them in the armed forces. In 1861, Frances Clayton disguised herself as a man. Calling herself Jack Williams, she fought alongside her husband Elmer Clayton in the Union armies during the Civil War. After Elmer was killed in 1862, she continued fighting and was wounded three times before she was discharged from the army the following year.

BATTALION OF DEATH
After the first Russian Revolution broke out in March 1917, morale dropped among Russian soldiers fighting Germany in World War I. In response, Maria Botchkareva formed a battalion of 2,000 volunteer women "to shame the men". About 300 of them fought bravely alongside men.

Gun and uniform given to the battalion by the Russian army

A soldier from the Women's Battalion of Death on parade

Sword wrapped by olive branch

Hebrew name of the force

Badge of the Israeli Defense Force

ISRAELI ARMED FORCES
When the state of Israel was created in 1948, women fought alongside men in the war against Arab armies. After the war, they were discharged from combat positions but continued to be drafted alongside men to serve in training and other noncombat units. Since the 1990s, however, they have been readmitted into front-line units, although combat roles remain voluntary.

Iraqi women on army
assault course

STRONG ENOUGH?
One of the main questions about women serving
in the armed forces, particularly in the army, was
whether they are physically and mentally strong
enough to fight. Increased physical training—as
undertaken by these Iraqi women soldiers at a US
training camp in Jordan—means that this issue is
no longer relevant. When these women have
graduated, they will return home to join a
female unit in the Iraqi army.

*Running over a pole improves
balance and coordination*

AK47 assault rifle

WOMEN GUERRILLAS
Women have often
fought in guerrilla
armies, particularly
those fighting for
independence from
foreign rule. One-third of the
soldiers fighting in the Eritrean
People's Liberation Front for
independence from Ethiopia were
women. They have continued to
play a major role in Eritrea's
armed services since the country
became independent in 1993.

IN THE LINE OF FIRE?
It is difficult to draw a definite line
between support and combat roles in the
army. This Spanish soldier is patrolling a
street market in Iraq. She could easily be
drawn into combat if an insurgent opened
fire against her and her fellow soldiers.
She is in uniform, but is she in combat?

Child soldiers

THE UNITED NATIONS CONVENTION of the Rights of the Child, agreed in 1989 and amended in 2002, requires countries "to ensure that persons below the age of 18 do not take a direct part in hostilities and that they are not compulsorily recruited into their armed forces." The laws of the International Criminal Court are even clearer, stating that it is a "war crime" to enlist children under the age of 15 into a national army. Despite this, the organization Human Rights Watch estimated in 2008 that at least 200,000 children under 18 were serving in combat roles for rebel groups or government forces in 17 different countries around the world. Children as young as eight are conscripted, robbing them of the chance of an education, and leaving them physically and emotionally damaged.

Figurine of a
Spartan warrior

SPARTAN BOYS

Boys from Sparta—an ancient Greek kingdom—were trained in military skills from an early age. They were taken from their mothers at the age of seven and brought up in packs, where they competed in mock fights. Their military and physical training continued until at the age 20, when they became eligible for a lifetime of military service.

BOY SCOUTS

In 1899–1900 the Boers besieged forces under the British commander Robert Baden-Powell at Mafeking during the Boer War in southern Africa. Baden-Powell formed the boys of the town who were too young to fight into the Mafeking Cadet Corps and used them to run messages for his troops. He used the Corps as a model for the Scouting Movement, an organization that he formed in 1907 to develop the mental and physical abilities of boys.

Young recruit to 3rd
Battalion, Duke of
Lancaster's Regiment,
British Army

UNDER AGE

Many young men have lied about their age in order to be allowed into the army. Private Valentine Joe Strudwick was only 13 when, in August 1914, Britain went to war against Germany. He gave a false age and enlisted in the Rifle Brigade. Private Strudwick was killed at Ypres in Belgium in January 1916, aged just 14 years 10 months, although his tombstone states that he was 15.

Gravestone of
Private Strudwick,
Essex Farm Cemetery,
Ypres, Belgium

YOUNG RECRUITS

The usual age to recruit young people into the armed services is 18. This is the age at which people are usually allowed to vote in elections. Some countries, including the US and Canada, allow children in at 17, and Britain allows them in aged 16½, although they cannot take part in military campaigns until they are 18.

Girl soldiers in FARC
(Revolutionary Armed
Forces of Colombia)

Child soldier of pro-
government Liberia
Peace Council militia

GIRL GUERRILLAS
It is estimated that more than 100,000 young girls are currently
fighting wars around the world. Since 1990, young girls have
fought in conflicts in 38 different countries. During the civil war in
the Democratic Republic of Congo in 1997–2006, girls were forced
to fight for the government as well as its guerrilla opponents.

AK47 assault rifle

CHILD GUERRILLAS
Most child soldiers fight for guerrilla groups
opposed to, or in some cases supporting, a national
government. During the bloody civil wars that have
ravaged Liberia, Sierra Leone, and Uganda since the 1980s,
guerrillas kidnapped children from their villages. They
preferred children since they are easier to control than
adults and can be trained to commit terrible atrocities.
Former child soldiers often suffer terrible nightmares and
need years of counseling to overcome feelings of guilt for
the appalling things they were forced to do.

Former child soldiers from
southern Sudan training to
be car mechanics in Kenya

REHABILITATION
Child soldiers have often known no other life but war
and find it hard to adjust to peace. In addition to
counseling to help them heal mentally, this group of
former child soldiers is being retrained to master auto
mechanics and other practical skills they can use to
make a peaceful living. Others are taught to read and
write for the first time in their lives.

Soldiers for peace

W**HEN YOU THINK OF A SOLDIER**, you think of a person who is trained to fight in war. But some soldiers work for peace. Ever since 1948, the United Nations (UN)—an international organization representing all the countries of the world—has deployed peacekeeping forces that keep warring nations apart, enforce ceasefires, and work to establish peace in troubled regions. The troops come from various member nations but work under orders from the UN, whose flag they fly and whose uniform they wear. As of 2008, the UN had completed 49 international missions and is currently undertaking a further 16, mainly in the Middle East and Africa.

THE BLUE BERET
United Nations troops wear a light-blue beret or helmet to identify themselves as peacekeepers, not hostile troops. The colored beret is so distinctive that UN troops are often called "the Blue Berets" or "Blue Helmets."

UN troops wearing light-blue berets and uniforms

UN armored personnel carrier

WHITE FOR PEACE
UN troops drive armored vehicles painted white. The color white is designed to stand out against most natural backgrounds. However, that also means that the vehicles are very visible and occasionally come under fire from an enemy that does not wish the UN to be present.

FIGHTING FOR PEACE
UN troops are mainly involved in peacekeeping, but in 1950 they fought a war after North Korea invaded its neighbor, South Korea. A UN vote condemned the attack and, although the Soviet Union and China did not vote, it was decided to send troops to protect South Korea. More than 500,000 troops from 16 nations fought under the UN flag until a ceasefire was declared in 1953.

Non-Violence sculpture outside the
UN headquarters in New York

*Knotted barrel symbolizes the UN's
peacekeeping mission*

UN FAILURES
The Blue Berets are not always successful in their task.
In 1993, 400 Dutch peacekeepers were sent to protect
Bosnian Muslims in the UN-designated safe haven of
Srebrenica. However, the Dutch were powerless to
resist when the Serb army overran the safe area in
1995, later killing more than 8,000 Muslims in the
worst atrocity in Europe since the end of World War II.

ROLE OF THE UN
The United Nations was set up at the end of World War II in 1945
as an international forum where countries could discuss issues of
concern to them all. It aims to stop wars between countries and work
toward peace, as well as achieving social progress and safeguarding
human rights. This sculpture of a knotted gun by Swedish artist
Fredrik Reuterswärd was given to the UN by Luxembourg in 1988.

*Watchtower gives good
view of terrain and keeps
the UN presence visible*

SUPERVISING A TRUCE
UN peacekeepers are often called in to supervise
a truce declared between two warring states. They
take up positions along the ceasefire line and watch
both sides to make sure they are not breaking the
terms of the truce or preparing to start
fighting again. The UN has had
peacekeepers on the Golan Heights
between Israel and Syria
since 1974.

NON-UN PEACEKEEPERS
Most peacekeeping operations in the world are organized
by the United Nations. A few, however, are independent
operations. In 1969, British troops were sent to keep the peace
between Protestants and Catholics in Northern Ireland,
a province of the United Kingdom. Increasingly drawn into
the conflict, they remained there until 2007.

POLICING THE WORLD
The UN is currently active
all across the world. It
has observed the conflict
in Georgia in the Caucasus
since 1993, policed the ceasefire
in Liberia, West Africa, since
2003, and attempted
to stabilize the
troubled island
of Haiti in the
Caribbean since
2004. Participating
troops are awarded
the UN Service Medal.

Tomorrow's soldier

IT IS DIFFICULT TO IMAGINE what tomorrow's soldiers will look like and how they will fight, but that has not stopped some governments from trying. The United States military is developing the Future Combat Systems project that will, among other things, create the Future Force Warrior (FFW). This futuristic concept will use cutting-edge technology to create a more effective soldier. Encased in extra-strong armor, and aware of everything around him, tomorrow's soldier will have improved protection, firepower, and military intelligence.

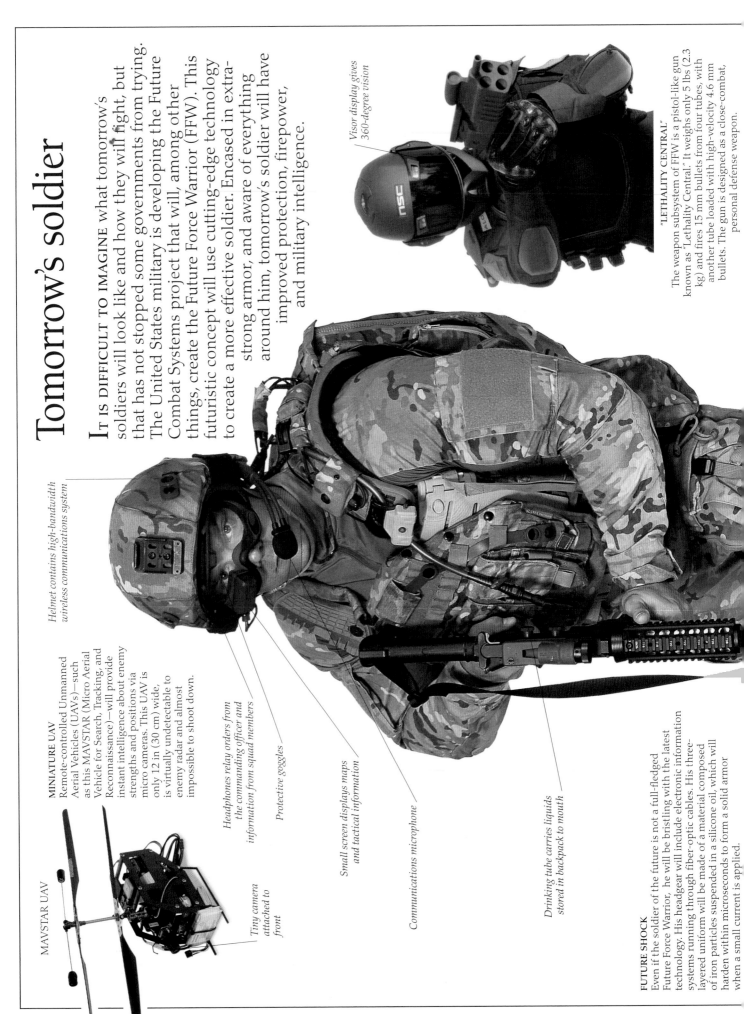

Visor display gives 360-degree vision

"LETHALITY CENTRAL"
The weapon subsystem of FFW is a pistol-like gun known as "Lethality Central." It weighs only 5 lbs (2.3 kg) and fires 15 mm bullets from four tubes, with another tube loaded with high-velocity 4.6 mm bullets. The gun is designed as a close-combat, personal defense weapon.

Helmet contains high-bandwidth wireless communications system

MINIATURE UAV
Remote-controlled Unmanned Aerial Vehicles (UAVs)—such as this MAVSTAR (Micro Aerial Vehicle for Search, Tracking, and Reconnaissance)—will provide instant intelligence about enemy strengths and positions via micro cameras. This UAV is only 12 in (30 cm) wide, is virtually undetectable to enemy radar and almost impossible to shoot down.

Headphones relay orders from the commanding officer and information from squad members

Protective goggles

Small screen displays maps and tactical information

Communications microphone

Drinking tube carries liquids stored in backpack to mouth

MAVSTAR UAV

Tiny camera attached to front

FUTURE SHOCK
Even if the soldier of the future is not a full-fledged Future Force Warrior, he will be bristling with the latest technology. His headgear will include electronic information systems running through fiber-optic cables. His three-layered uniform will be made of a material composed of iron particles suspended in a silicone oil, which will harden within microseconds to form a solid armor when a small current is applied.

Uniform contains a microclimate conditioning system, which heats or cools its wearer by circulating hot or cold fluids through narrow tubes

ROBOT SOLDIERS

Speech-controlled surveillance robots will play an increasing role in tomorrow's conflicts, replacing soldiers in dangerous tasks such as mine detection, bomb disposal, and close-quarters reconnaissance. Robot soldiers will act as the ears and eyes of combat troops, and could reduce casualties by allowing commanders to assess potential risks before sending in humans.

Cargo pallets can be unloaded automatically

Oshkosh PLS unmanned ground vehicle

UNMANNED VEHICLES

The radio-controlled, unmanned military vehicles of tomorrow will range from tanks to supply-carrying trucks, such as this one. It can deliver weapons and equipment directly to the combat zone and even unload them in the right place, without the need for soldiers, who are freed up for other tasks.

Powered legs can run twice their normal speed

Cables carry power to motors in exoskeleton

Lower body exoskeleton

EXOSKELETON

An exoskeleton is a machine attached to a person to increase his strength and range of movement. Powered by a battery worn in the soldier's backpack, the exoskeleton could help a soldier move and lift heavy weights, such as large rocket launchers or mortars. This soldier is wearing an exoskeleton on his legs, improving their power and endurance.

Timeline

Ever since soldiers first took up arms to fight for their leader or country, they have been involved in battles. Some battles are small-scale events involving only a few hundred soldiers and lasting just a few hours. Others involve many thousands of men fighting over the course of several days or weeks. Here are some of the many famous battles that have taken place throughout history.

Alexander the Great fighting the Persians, 333 BCE

Crusades, 1187

c. 1275 BCE: KADESH
The chariot armies of the Egyptians and the Hittites (a people from Anatolia, modern-day Turkey) clashed in western Syria in this fast-moving battle. It ended in an agreement between the two sides to stop fighting—the world's first recorded peace treaty.

490 BCE: MARATHON
Persian invaders were defeated by Athenian hoplites at Marathon near Athens in Greece. Legend has it that a runner carried news of the victory to Athens—the first marathon run.

333 BCE: ISSUS
Alexander the Great met the Persian army at Issus in northern Syria on a narrow plain. His Macedonian cavalry swept all before them, encircling the Persian infantry. The Persian king, Darius, escaped, but Alexander completed his conquest of the Persian empire two years later.

216 BCE: CANNAE
During the Punic Wars between Rome and Carthage, Hannibal of Carthage attacked the Romans at Cannae, southeast Italy. 50,000 Romans were killed in the one-day battle. Hannibal attempted for 16 years to conquer Rome, but ultimately failed.

52 BCE: ALESIA
The Roman general Julius Caesar invaded Gaul (France) and besieged the Gallic forces at Alesia. A relief force came to the rescue before Caesar's infantry combined to drive them off.

636 CE: YARMUK
Muslim Arab forces met a Christian Byzantine army by the Yarmuk River in Syria. A massive sandstorm allowed the Arab armies to mount a surprise attack and defeat the Byzantines.

732: POITIERS
A Muslim army from Spain invaded southern France. Near Poitiers, Frankish knights formed a tightly packed square that they defended with sword and spear, eventually forcing the Muslim army to withdraw.

751: TALAS RIVER
A Muslim army advancing east through central Asia clashed with a Chinese army on the Talas River. Turkish horsemen defected to the Muslims from the Chinese during the battle, resulting in a Muslim victory. This ended Chinese rule in Central Asia and brought the region under Islamic control.

1066: HASTINGS
An army of around 7,000 men under William of Normandy (the Conqueror) met the 9,000-strong Saxon army of King Harold of England. Harold was killed, giving the throne of England to William.

1187: HATTIN
During the Crusades—the wars between Christians and Muslims for control of the Holy Land—a Muslim army under the leadership of Saladin defeated the Christian Crusader army.

1346: CRÉCY
Edward III of England invaded France in 1337 at the start of the 100 Years' War. His army was later trapped at Crécy by a far larger French force. The English fired volleys of arrows at the French cavalry to kill their horses, forcing the knights to dismount and fight on foot. More than 4,000 French died, but just 200 English.

1386: KOSOVO
The Ottoman Turkish advance into Europe came up against a Serb force in Kosovo. Both Ottoman and Serb rulers were killed in the battle, which was won by the Ottomans, bringing southeast Europe under their control for more than 500 years.

1415: AGINCOURT
In the last stages of the 100 Years' War, Henry V of England invaded France, where his force of 6,000 men was stopped by a 25,000-strong French army. The English longbowmen won the day, as about 5,000 Frenchmen were killed, but only 300–400 English died.

1532: CAJAMARCA
The Spanish conquistador Francisco Pizarro and around 200 men landed in Peru and headed for the Inca emperor Atahualpa's base at Cajamarca, where they confronted an Inca army 40,000 strong. Using superior weapons, the Spanish captured Atahualpa, whose empire soon fell to Pizarro.

1576: ALCAZARQUIVIR
The Portuguese king Sebastian invaded Morocco in support of its deposed king but his army was routed by a far superior Arab army, one of the few times a European army has met defeat at the hands of an African force.

1631: FIRST BREITENFIELD
In 1618, the Thirty Years' War broke out between Protestant and Catholic forces in the Holy Roman Empire (roughly modern-day Germany). Sweden entered on the Protestant side in 1630, and under Gustavus Adolphus scored a major victory by attacking the flank of the Catholic army late in the battle.

Waterloo medal, 1815

1704: BLENHEIM
The War of the Spanish Succession (1702–13) allied France and Spain against Austria, England, and the Netherlands. An army under English Duke of Marlborough and Prince Eugene of Savoy confronted the French in Bavaria. The French line was overextended, allowing Marlborough to split it apart and win the battle.

1757: LEUTHEN
Led by King Frederick the Great, the Prussians defeated the Austrians at Leuthen. Frederick pretended to attack the Austrian right flank but then quickly moved troops to their left flank. His "walking batteries" of infantry overwhelmed the enemy.

German
World War II
firefigher's
helmet

1759: QUEBEC
The struggle between Britain and France for dominance in North America reached its climax in 1759, when the British, under General Wolfe, attacked Quebec, capital of French Canada. Wolfe scaled the cliffs by the Quebec River upstream from the city. He attacked from there, taking the French by surprise and winning an easy victory, giving Britain control of Canada.

1777: SARATOGA
One year after the American Declaration of Independence, the British attempted to cut the American colonies in two by advancing from Canada down the Hudson River to New York. The Americans surrounded the British at Saratoga and forced them to surrender.

1805: AUSTERLITZ
French emperor Napoleon Bonaparte's greatest victory took place at Austerlitz in what is now the Czech Republic, where he defeated a combined Austrian and Russian army. Further victories at Jena and Wagram confirmed Napoleon's dominance of Europe.

1815: WATERLOO
Napoleon's final battle occurred south of Brussels, where he attacked an Anglo-Dutch army led by the Duke of Wellington and a Prussian army under Blücher. After heavy fighting, the French lines broke and fled, pursued by Prussian cavalry.

1863: GETTYSBURG
This unplanned three-day battle during the American Civil War ended with the Confederate army retreating in disarray. They had been attacked by Union troops after entering Gettysburg in search of shoes.

1914: TANNENBERG
At the start of World War I, the Russians invaded German East Prussia, where they were encircled and slaughtered by German artillery. About 140,000 out of 150,000 Russian troops were either killed or injured.

1916: THE SOMME
The British began an artillery bombardment of German lines in an attempt to break the stalemate of World War I. The tactic failed and the British suffered 57,460 casualties on the first day of battle. When the battle ended four months later, the British finally captured targets they had planned to seize on the first day.

Israeli troops and Egyptian POWs,
Six Day War, 1967

1942: EL ALAMEIN
During World War II, German forces under Rommel occupied North Africa. General Montgomery organized an Allied offensive that began with an artillery bombardment of German lines. New Zealand troops cleared a way through German minefields and the Allies won after 13 days of fighting.

1942–43: STALINGRAD
Invading German troops attacked the Russian city of Stalingrad, forcing the Russians back to a thin strip of city. They were soon surrounded by a Russian army. The Germans eventually surrendered, suffering more than 500,000 casualties. Russian losses were even higher.

1943: KURSK
The biggest tank battle in history took place in Russia, as 3,500 Soviet tanks punched a hole in the German line held by 2,700 tanks. Casualties on both sides were immense, but Soviet firepower won the day in a battle that shifted the balance of World War II away from Germany and toward the Soviet Union.

1967: SIX-DAY WAR
Israel launched a massive attack on the Egyptian air force, destroying four-fifths of it. Attacks against Jordanian and Syrian air forces followed before Israel invaded the Egyptian-held Sinai peninsula, the Jordanian West Bank, and the Syrian Golan Heights, doubling the size of Israeli-held territory.

1968: TET OFFENSIVE
North Vietnamese troops launched a surprise attack against South Vietnamese cities during the long-running war in Vietnam. The offensive convinced many Americans that they could not win the war, which they were fighting on the side of the South Vietnamese. In 1973, the US withdrew completely from the conflict, which was won by the communist North in 1975.

1990–91: KUWAIT
In 1990, Iraq invaded oil-rich Kuwait. The following year, a US-led force made up of troops from 29 different countries began a six-week aerial bombardment of Iraq before ground troops liberated Kuwait in a four-day battle. It was marked by the use of hi-tech weaponry and stealth bombers able to avoid radar detection.

2004: FALLUJAH
US Marines and Iraqi government troops attacked insurgents in the city of Fallujah in central Iraq. The US forces eventually drove the insurgents out of the city after a nine-day battle. The US Marines described the battle as the heaviest conflict they had been involved in since the Vietnam War.

US Marines, Vietnam War, 1968

Portraying the soldier

NOVELISTS, POETS, FILMMAKERS, and painters have all depicted soldiers in their works. Their portrayals have shown some soldiers as heroes, others as normal people caught up in tragic events. These works show fictional and real soldiers. They help us understand what it is like to fight as a soldier.

BOOKS

War has always provided drama, conflict, and tragedy to inspire novelists. They have written about the experiences of soldiers, and of how people cope with extreme events.

THE ILIAD
Homer's epic poem, dating from the 8th century BCE, tells the story of Greek warrior Achilles' many adventures during the Trojan War. It is one of the first works of fiction ever to be written down.

THE THREE MUSKETEERS
Alexander Dumas' 1844 novel recounts the adventures of a young man in 17th-century France who sets out to become a Musketeer of the Guard in the king's household.

WAR AND PEACE
One of the world's most famous novels, *War and Peace* was completed by Russian author Leo Tolstoy in 1869, and is set during Napoleon's invasion of Russia in 1812.

THE RED BADGE OF COURAGE
Using a ground-breaking realistic style, Stephen Crane's 1895 novel describes the experience of a 19-year-old Civil War soldier as he encounters the cruelty of war.

ALL QUIET ON THE WESTERN FRONT
This novel of 1929 by German author Erich Remarque describes the cruelty of war from the point of a view of a 20-year-old soldier. It contributed to antiwar feelings of the time.

POETRY

Some of the greatest war poetry was written by soldiers serving in World War I. Most did not write about victories or heroism, but about the horror of war.

THE BRITISH WAR POETS
The major British poets of World War I were Rupert Brooke (1887–1915), Robert Graves (1895–1985), Wilfred Owen (1893–1918), and Siegfried Sassoon (1886–1967). Brooke and Owen were killed during the war.

ARCHIBALD MACLEISH
An artillery captain during World War I, US poet MacLeish (1892–1982) published a book of poems in honor of his brother, who was killed in the war.

Rupert Brooke

JOHN MCCRAE
A Canadian field surgeon, McCrae (1872–1918) wrote "In Flanders Field," one of the best-known poems of World War I.

FILMS

Stories about warfare have been central to the movies ever since the first silent films were produced at the end of the 19th century. World War II and the Vietnam War are particularly popular themes.

A film still from *Henry V*, 1944

HENRY V (1944)
British actor Laurence Olivier directed and starred in *Henry V*, a film version of William Shakespeare's play. Although the events take place in 1415 during the Hundred Years War between England and France, the film was intended to boost British morale during the final stages of World War II.

THE SEVEN SAMURAI (1954)
This Japanese classic directed by Akira Kurosawa tells the story of seven *ronin*— samurai warriors not bound to any lord— who defend a village from bandits. The film explores the samurai's code of honor. It was remade in the US as a western, with cowboys instead of samurai, in a film called *The Magnificent Seven*.

PATHS OF GLORY (1957)
Based on a novel by Humphrey Cobb, this film by director Stanley Kubrick tells the story of three French soldiers who are tried unfairly for cowardice during World War I. Although it is often considered an "antiwar" movie, Kubrick felt that the film's real targets were authoritarianism and ignorance.

GALLIPOLI (1981)
The story of two young Australian sprinters who join up at the start of World War I. They are sent to fight in Turkey, where they are caught up in the horrors of the Gallipoli campaign. Director Peter Weir based the battle scenes on real events in this gripping tale starring a young Mel Gibson.

GETTYSBURG (1993)
An epic dramatization of the decisive Battle of Gettysburg during the Civil War. The story of the three-day battle is told from the point of view of both sides, and the action is re-created by a cast of thousands on the exact location of the real battle.

WAR GAMES

In recent years, interest in soldiers from different periods in history has grown considerably. People want to find out how soldiers in history lived and fought, what uniforms they wore, and which guns they carried.

REENACTMENTS
A good way to experience exactly what it was like to take part in a major battle is to stage a reenactment. People dress up in the uniforms of the time and reenact every stage of the battle. In the United States, Civil War reenactment has become increasingly popular in recent years, with great attention paid to the accuracy of uniforms and weapons. In 1998, a reenactment of the Battle of Gettysburg drew more than 15,000 participants. Reenactment societies perform in front of large crowds and are often used as extras in battle scenes for films and TV shows.

TOY SOLDIERS
During the 19th century, boys used to collect miniature tin soldiers. They arranged them in formation and pretended they were fighting a major battle. Today's toy soldiers are collected by both children and adults. The larger G. I. Joe dolls are also popular, since they can be dressed in many different uniforms.

STATUES

Sculptures of soldiers are most commonly found on war memorials. Most cities have public sculptures of soldiers to commemorate a country's past conflicts.

THE TERRA-COTTA ARMY
Qin Shi Huang (ruled 221–210 BCE) was the first emperor of China. He ordered 8,000 soldiers to be sculpted out of terra-cotta (clay) to form an army to protect him in his tomb.

TRAJAN'S COLUMN
The 100-ft (30-m) tall column was erected in Rome to commemorate Emperor Trajan's victories against the Dacians in 101–106 CE. Around the column are scenes depicting the Roman army preparing for war.

MARINE CORPS WAR MEMORIAL
Located near the Arlington National Cemetery in Virginia, this statue depicts the raising of the flag at Iwo Jima and is dedicated to all US Marines who have died in battle.

North Korean war statue, Pyongyang, North Korea, built in 1972

ART

Death of General Wolfe by Benjamin West

Art galleries are full of paintings depicting soldiers. Most depict famous victories, but modern painters have concentrated on the life of the common soldier.

HENRY MOORE
During World War II, British sculptor Moore (1898–1986) produced a series of drawings showing Londoners sheltering from the Blitz—the bombing of their city.

PABLO PICASSO
On April 26, 1937, German bombers attacked the town of Guernica in the Basque Country, killing hundreds of people. The Germans were supporting the Nationalist forces of General Franco during the Spanish Civil War of 1936–39. Spanish artist Picasso (1881–1973) painted a vast canvas depicting the event. It is one of the most famous antiwar paintings ever created, and hangs in the Reina Sofia Museum in Madrid, Spain.

FRANCISCO DE GOYA
The Spanish artist Goya (1746–1828) lived during the French occupation of Spain from 1807 to 1814. His paintings and drawings depict the brutalities committed by both sides in the war. His most famous war painting, *The Third of May 1808*, shows a French firing squad shooting dead citizens of Madrid who had rebelled against French rule. The painting is in the Prado Museum in Madrid, Spain.

POSTERS

Propaganda is the deliberate attempt to influence people to behave the way you want them to. Governments produce propaganda posters to influence both their own citizens and those of their enemies.

RECRUITMENT POSTERS
During World War I, rival governments issued recruitment posters encouraging young men to enlist in the armed services. The British used the image of famous war hero Lord Kitchener to inspire men to enlist. Posters and other forms of advertising, including television, are used today when recruits are required to keep peacetime armies up to strength.

THE HOME FRONT
Posters are a good way to get information across to civilians. During World War II, the British government used posters to urge people to grow their own food and to observe the blackout—making sure that no lights could be seen outside their houses that might help enemy bombers find their targets.

INSPIRING PATRIOTISM
The Soviet Union produced a huge number of posters during World War II showing heroic soldiers and civilians defending their land. The Soviets suffered more than any other country during the war—25 million of their citizens were killed—so it was crucial to maintain morale in any way they could.

US Marines recruiting poster

Find out more

THERE ARE LOTS OF WAYS TO find out more about soldiers and the role they play. Ask older members of your family if they have been a soldier or know anyone who is— they will have plenty of facts and stories to tell you. You can also search your school or local library for books about soldiers, and visit military museums and army camps when they have open days. Look for television documentaries about life in the army and check the websites recommended opposite—there is a mass of information online.

VISITING MUSEUMS
Military museums, such as this one in Beijing, China, are great places to find out more about army life. They contain displays of weaponry and military equipment, uniforms, and medals, as well as many records of historic wars and battles. They also consider the impact wars had on the nations that fought them.

Chinese troops help a young girl along an assault course

OPEN DAYS
Most army camps have open days when the general public can tour the camp, see parades and other displays by soldiers, and inspect the weaponry that they use. Such tours are a good way to find out more about where a soldier lives and what his day-to-day life involves.

Open day at a military camp in Hong Kong

US Marine Corps War Memorial

WAR MEMORIALS
Major wars and battles are remembered with memorials, such as this bronze statue erected near Washington, D.C., to honor US marines who have died in battle. It is based on a famous photograph taken of marines raising the US flag on Iwo Jima in 1945 after the island had been captured from the Japanese. Memorials can tell us much about a war and the soldiers who fought in it.

Village war memorial, Desertines, Mayenne, France

LOCAL WAR MEMORIALS
In World War I, many men left their hometowns never to return. In most cases, they had been ordinary civilians, and local communities were shocked by their loss. They erected memorials listing those from their towns who had died fighting for their country. Many thousands of British and French towns have memorials that are the focus of Remembrance Day commemorations every November.

BATTLEFIELD TOURS
Many battle sites are open to the public and have guided tours and exhibitions explaining the course of the battle itself. Miles of tunnels were dug by the Vietnamese in the 1960s and 1970s to hide from US troops and to protect themselves against bombing raids during their lengthy war. The tunnels are now open to the public, but they are a tight fit for all but the slimmest people!

USEFUL WEBSITES

- About.com US Military site, featuring charts of ranks and insignia and a directory of modern weapons: **usmilitary.about.com**
- US Army official website: **www.army.mil**
- National World War II Museum website, featuring historical photos and an interactive timeline of the war: **www.nationalww2museum.org**
- PBS's Civil War site, where you can examine details of historical photos and even make your own movie: **www.pbs.org/civilwar/**
- Knights in Central Park, a virtual tour of the Metropolitan Museum's outstanding arms and armor collection: **www.metmuseum.org/explore/knights/home.html**
- Online database of the more than 58,000 names on the Vietnam Veterans' memorial Wall in Washington, D.C.: **thewall-usa.com**
- US Center of Military History, with images and extracts from military books on every conflict the US has been involved in: **www.history.army.mil**

Places to visit

NATIONAL INFANTRY MUSEUM, COLUMBUS, OHIO
- Slated to open in Spring 2009, this museum will focus on the lives of ordinary soldiers, from the Revolutionary War to today.

ARLINGTON NATIONAL CEMETERY, ARLINGTON, VIRGINIA
- More than 300,000 people are buried in this famous military cemetery, including veterans from all major wars. The Tomb of the Unknowns is a popular destination for tourists.

GETTYSBURG BATTLEFIELD, GETTYSBURG, PENNSYLVANIA
- Tour the site of the Civil War's Battle of Gettysburg, which now features a new museum and visitor center.

NATIONAL WORLD WAR II MEMORIAL, WASHINGTON, D.C.,
- A memorial dedicated to the 16 million men and women from the US who served in World War II, open to the public 24 hours a day
- A large site covering 7 acres (3 hectares) of parkland

CALIFORNIA STATE MILITARY MUSEUM, SACRAMENTO, CALIFORNIA
- California's official military museum features artifacts from the age of the conquistadors to the present day.

THE METROPOPLITAN MUSEUM, NEW YORK, NEW YORK
- The Met boasts one of the world's finest collections of arms and armor, with objects ranging from 400 BCE to the 19th century.

VIETNAM VETERANS' MEMORIAL, WASHINGTON, D.C.
- Completed in 1993, this memorial's central feature its the Memorial Wall, which contains a list of more than 58,000 servicemen who were killed in the Vietnam War.

SPRINGFIELD ARMORY, SPRINGFIELD, MASSACHUSETTS
- For almost two centuries, the Springfield Armory served as an important weapons manufacturer for the US military. The site now serves as a museum, featuring many historical weapons and a Junior Ranger area for kids.

TEXAS MILITARY FORCES MUSEUM, AUSTIN, TEXAS
- This museum focuses on the soldiers of the Lone Star State, including those who fought in the famous battles of the Texas Revolution.

CANADIAN WAR MUSEUM, OTTOWA, ONTARIO, CANADA
- The Canadian War Museum features extensive exhibits covering Canada's long military history, starting with early conflicts between Europeans and First Nations tribes.

WAR GRAVES
The brutality of war and its terrible cost to human life are made real when you visit one of the vast graveyards in western Europe. Thousands of troops who were killed during both world wars are buried in these cemeteries.

Tyne Cot Cemetery, Belgium, containing graves of 10,000 soldiers killed at Ypres in World War I

Glossary

AMPHIBIOUS Able to work on both water and land.

APC Armored Personnel Carrier—a lightly armed, armored fighting vehicles used to transport infantry on the battlefield.

ARMISTICE Agreement between opposing sides to cease fire while a peace agreement is negotiated.

Israeli Achzarit APC

ARSENAL Store or collection of arms, ammunition, and other military equipment.

ARTILLERY Guns, cannons, howitzers, mortars, and other heavy weapons with a large caliber that are moved around using motorized vehicles. Artillery also refers to the troops or army units that use such weapons.

BARRACKS Buildings used to accommodate and train soldiers.

BARREL The tube of a gun, normally made of metal, through which the bullet is fired.

BATTALION A fighting unit of an army, usually consisting of about 900 troops. Each battalion is split into seven or eight companies. A group of battalions is called a regiment or brigade.

BULLET A solid metal projectile, usually with a lead core, that is fired by a gun.

CALIBER Internal diameter (bore) of a gun barrel or diameter of a shell or bullet, used to describe firearms and ammunition.

CAMOUFLAGE Disruptive pattern on equipment, uniforms, and face paint worn by soldiers, designed to break up their shape and conceal them against the natural background.

US Marines performing a drill

CANNON A form of artillery that fires heavy projectiles using explosives.

CAVALRY Originally soldiers on horseback; now soldiers using motorized transportation such as tanks.

CENSOR Person who checks letters and other documents and removes information from them if it might, in wartime, be useful to an enemy.

CHILD SOLDIER Soldier aged under 18—the minimum age any soldier should be sent into combat, according to the UN, which considers it a war crime to use soldiers aged under 15.

CIVILIAN Person whose main occupation is civil (nonmilitary).

COLOR Flag of an army unit.

COMMISSIONED OFFICER A soldier in official command of a military unit, who has normally received training in leadership at a military academy.

COMPANY A unit of between 75 and 200 soldiers, formed of several platoons.

CONSCRIPT Someone who is required by law to join the army, often against his will.

Model of a hoplite helmet

CONSCRIPTION A national plan to recruit soldiers into the army forcibly. In the US, this system is known as the Draft.

CORPS A group of soldiers within one of the armed services that has a particular function, such as artillery or signals. Also used to refer to certain branches of service, such as the US Marine Corps.

COURT MARTIAL Military court that tries soldiers and other military personnel accused of offenses under military law.

DRESS UNIFORM Formal ceremonial uniform of a soldier worn on parades and special occasions.

DRILL Repetitive marching on a parade ground and other exercises that teach a soldier discipline and obedience.

Longbowmen

ENLIST To join the armed services, either as a volunteer or a draftee.

FIREARM A weapon, such as a rifle or cannon, that shoots projectiles at high speed using a controlled explosion.

FLANK The side of a military formation, such as a line of troops.

FORMATION The formal arrangement of a group of troops in a line or block.

FRIENDLY FIRE Firing mistakenly directed at soldiers by their own side.

FRONT LINE The border with enemy armies or territories, where the fighting is.

GENEVA CONVENTION An international agreement laying down the rules governing the treatment of prisoners of war. By 2006, 193 countries had agreed to the convention.

GRENADE A small explosive weapon that is thrown by hand or fired longer distances by a grenade launcher.

GUERRILLA A soldier in a guerrilla army, a small-scale group of armed men and women, often politically motivated, who specialize in sabotage and hit-and-run attacks. The word "guerrilla" comes from the Spanish for "small war."

HOPLITE Heavily armed foot soldier from ancient Greece.

INFANTRY Soldiers who fight on foot.

INSURGENCY Armed uprising against an unpopular government or occupying foreign army.

INTELLIGENCE Military information about the enemy or potential enemy.

KNIGHT Warrior of a high social status, who fought on horseback. The term is normally used to describe mounted soldiers in medieval wars fought between 800 and 1600 CE.

M16A1 assault rifle

LEGION Unit of the Roman army made up of infantry and supporting cavalry and numbering 3,000–6,000 men.

LONGBOW Large bow used during the Middle Ages. It was usually made of yew wood and could fire arrows up to 1,000 ft (300 m) away. Soldiers specially trained to shoot a longbow were known as longbowmen.

MANEUVERS Large-scale military exercises involving infantry and cavalry divisions, often in a simulation of battlefield conditions. Maneuvers may involve the armies of several different countries.

MARINE Soldier who fights from the sea.

MASCOT Animal or object considered to bring good luck to a regiment or army unit.

MEDAL Award given to a soldier for service in a war or campaign or for outstanding bravery in the face of the enemy.

MERCENARY Hired soldier who fights only for money.

MESS A room where soldiers eat and relax.

MILITARY LAW Legal system for members of the armed services, covering such issues as military discipline, commands, and duties.

MORALE The level of confidence and optimism of a person or group of people.

MORTAR Artillery weapon that fires shells at a high trajectory or angle of fire that explode on impact.

MUSKET Long-barreled, muzzle-loading shoulder gun used by infantry between the 15th and 18th centuries. A soldier who used a musket was known as a musketman, or musketeer.

MUZZLE The front end of a gun barrel.

NCO Noncommissioned officer appointed from the ranks to command a group of soldiers.

Mortar

PARADE GROUND Large open square in a barracks where soldiers learn drill and other exercises.

PARATROOPER Soldier trained in parachuting to operate as part of an airborne force.

PHALANX Ancient Greek battle formation of hoplites presenting long spears from behind a wall of overlapping shields.

PLATOON Unit of troops usually consisting of three sections, or about 30 soldiers.

POW Short for "Prisoner Of War," a soldier or civilian captured in wartime. Most but not all POWs are members of the armed forces.

PROJECTILE An object designed to be thrown or fired through the air, such as a spear, bullet, arrow, or shell.

PROPAGANDA The organized distribution of information or ideas using posters, movies, television, or other media, in order to persuade people to act or think in a particular way. In wartime, this may be done to improve morale.

RANK The different levels of the army. The word often refers to the lower levels only, excluding the officers.

RATIONS Fixed allowance of food given to soldiers in the field.

RECONNAISSANCE Inspection of an enemy's position, activities, numbers, and resources, often undertaken in secret. Also known as scouting.

RECRUIT Person who joins the army, either as a volunteer or a draftee.

REGIMENT Army unit based on a region or historical association consisting of several battalions.

RELIEF FORCE Group of soldiers sent to replace or help another group under attack or under siege.

RESERVES Soldiers who have received some military training but are held back until they are required to fight. Ex-soldiers may be required to serve as reserves for a fixed period after leaving the armed forces.

RIFLE Firearm with a long barrel that has a spirally grooved interior. This spins the bullet as it is fired and gives it greater accuracy.

ROUT Overwhelming military defeat.

SAMURAI Japanese medieval knight, born into a military family and trained to fight from a young age.

SABOTAGE The destruction of buildings and facilities that are important to an enemy, such as factories, dams, or bridges. Often this is done by small local groups planting bombs.

SECTION Smallest unit of the army, consisting of around 10 men.

SHELL An object fired by a tank, field gun, or other heavy artillery, that contains explosives designed to detonate when it hits its target.

SIEGE Military blockade, often lasting many months, carried out to capture a town, castle, or military stronghold.

SPECIAL FORCES Soldiers trained to undertake highly dangerous, secret operations against enemy forces.

STANDARD Flag or distinctive emblem of an army unit, which was carried into battle.

STRATEGY The plans made by high-level officers concerning the operations of a whole army.

SURVEILLANCE Close observation of an enemy group to pinpoint its position and strength, often undertaken in secret.

TACTICS The plans made for small units of men, before and during a battle.

TANK A heavily armored vehicle, usually with a large-caliber main gun mounted on a rotating turret.

TERRORIST Person who uses illegal methods, such as planting bombs in public places, as a means to achieve his or her goals.

TRENCH WARFARE A slow and grueling form of warfare in which the opposing sides both dig lines of long, narrow ditches, called trenches, to face each other along a front line.

TRUCE A temporary agreement to stop fighting, allowing time to negotiate a treaty (a formal agreement) to end a war.

UAV Unmanned Aerial Vehicle—an aircraft that is flown using remote control.

VOLLEY Simultaneous discharge of a number of guns or cannons.

VOLUNTEER A person who joins the army by their own free will.

Samurai sword

Index

Acknowledgments

Dorling Kindersley would like to thank:
David Ekholm–JAlbum, Sunita Gahir, Steve Setford, Su St. Louis, Lisa Stock, & Bulent Yusuf for the clip art; Sue Nicholson & Su St. Louis for the wall chart; Richard Beatty for proofreading Margaret Parrish & John Searcy for Americanization.

The Publishers would like to thank the following for their kind permission to reproduce their photographs:

(Key: a-above; b-below/bottom; c-center; l-left; r-right; t-top)

akg-images: 30tl; British Library, London 52tl; Erich Lessing 23cb; Musée de l'Armée, Paris 48cl; Ullstein Bild 36tl; **Alamy Images:** Sandra Baker 51cr; Suzy Bennett 45br; Caro 37crb, 59br; Mary Evans Picture Library 29bl, 36cl; Simon Hathaway 69tl; The London Art Archive 56tl; North Wind Picture Archives 26tr; North Winds Picture Archives 24bl; Popperfoto 85bl; Alistair Scott 58bl; Visions of America, LLC 48-49bc; Terence Waeland 51l; Gary Were 68br; World History Archive 29crb; **The Art Archive:** Archaeological Museum, Istanbul / Dagli Orti 64cl; Bibliothèque Nationale, Paris 3tr, 22tr; Musée Condé, Chantilly / Dagli Orti 64tr; National Archives, Washington, D.C. 19c; US Naval Museum, Washington 3tl (Left), 49tr (Left); **Berkeley Robotics Laboratory, University of California:** 63cl; **The Bridgeman Art Library:** Imperial War Museum, London 48tl (Medal of Honour); National Army Museum, London 15bc; **The Civil War Home Page (www.civil-war.net):** 32b; **Corbis:** 17bl, 41cl; Bettmann 8tl, 10br, 30br, 47tl, 54tr; China Features / Li Gang 38b; Geoffrey Clements 20tl; Steven Clevenger 46tl; CNP / Ron Sachs 53b; Dallas Morning News / Cheryl Diaz Meyer 19tl; EPA 7br, 43bl; EPA / Jim Hollander 38b; Tim Graham 50tl; Hulton-Deutsch Collection 30cl; Ed Kashi 61bl; Benjamin Lowy 31tl; Michael Nicholson 66cra; Reuters / Ceerwan Aziz 55tl; Reuters / Fayaz Kabli 51br; Reuters / Hassan Atef 23tl;

Reuters / Nikola Solic 57br; Reuters / U.S. Air Force 37cla; Michael St Maur Sheil 69bl; Leif Skoogfors 37cra; Stapleton Collection 47br; Swim Ink 2, LLC 67br; Sygma / China Features 6bl; Sygma / Patrick Robert 18br, 59l; Sygma / Robert Patrick 53t; David Turnley 9tr; Underwood & Underwood 56bl; Michael S. Yamashita 16cr; ZUMA / Mark Richards 54b; **By kind permission of the Cuneo Estate:** 46bl; **DK Images:** Courtesy of the 95th Rifles and Re-Enactment Living History Unit / Geoff Brightling 2ca, 21tc; The British Museum, London / Nick Nicholls 58tl; Confederate Memorial Hall, New Orleans / Dave King 19br; Courtesy of the D-Day Museum, Portsmouth / Andrew Shennan 17c; Courtesy of Mark Dennis / Geoff Dann 15cl; Felix deWeldon / Giles Stokoe 68bl; Courtesy of David Edge / Geoff Dann 4tc, 8bc; Courtesy of the Gettysburg National Military Park, PA / Dave King 2cla, 30br; Courtesy of the Imperial War Museum, London 2tr, 11tl, 25bl; Courtesy of the Imperial War Museum, London / Geoff Dann 4tr, 31bl, 41cr; Courtesy of the Imperial War Museum, London / Andy Crawford 2br, 8cl, 23cra, 23tr, 52bl, 52bc, 52cb, 52cl, 65cl; Courtesy of Kate Howey and Elgan Loane of Kentree Ltd, Ireland / Andy Crawford 22br, 22br; Courtesy of Denis Lassus, Paris / Tim Ridley 34-35cl; Judith Miller / Wallis and Wallis 3tl (Right), 49tr (Right); Courtesy of the Collections du Musées Nationale de la Légion d'Honneur / Max Alexander 48tl (Légion d'Honneur); National Museums of Scotland / Scottish United Services Museum, Edinburgh Castle / Geoff Dann 4cra, 15bc, 15t, 17r, 71bl; Courtesy of the Powell-Cotton Museum, Kent 3bl, 25cl; Courtesy of the Royal Green Jackets Museum, Winchester / Geoff Dann 48tl (Victoria Cross), 64br; Courtesy of the Royal Marines Museum, Portsmouth / Andrew Shennan 4clb, 38tl; Courtesy of the Royal Marines, Poole / Dave Rudkin 4bl, 39bl; Courtesy of the U.S. Army Heritage and Education Center - Military History Institute / Dave King 19tr; Courtesy of the University Museum of Newcastle / Tina Chambers and James Stevenson 2cr, 24tl; Courtesy of the Wallace

Collection, London / Geoff Dann 9l; Courtesy of the Wallace Collection, London / Andy Crawford 71c; **Getty Images:** AFP 40bl, 60clb; AFP / Aamir Qureshi 7cl; AFP / Ahmad Al-Rubaye 9cr; AFP / Awad Awad 12bl; AFP / Eric Feferberg 39tl; AFP / Goh Chai Hin 13br; AFP / Jack Guez 11br; AFP / Mychele Daniau 35bl; AFP / Ramzi Haidar 42bl; AFP / Sanka Vidanagama 14b; Aurora / Curtis Johnson 25cr; Natalie Behring-Chisholm 13tl; The Bridgeman Art Library 6cl, 7tr; Central Press 53cra; Fox Photos / Reg Speller 16bl; Stuart Franklin 3cr, 29cra; Tim Graham 11bl; Bert Hardy 60br; Hulton Archive 40cl; Keystone 45cr; Marco di Lauro 43tr, 49br; Scott Nelson 29t; Erik de Castro-Pool 20b; Popperfoto 49bl; Ryan Pyle 7bl; Reza 55cl; Peter Rogers 68tl; David Silverman 25tc; Time Life Pictures / Time Life Pictures 65bl; Time Life Pictures / Mansell 31tr; Time Life Pictures / Thomas Hartwell 27tr; U.S. Navy / Kittie Vanden-Bosch 31c; Ian Waldie 41br; **Imperial War Museum:** Sgt. Christie / B 05288 35tr; **Provided by the www.israelimilitary.com – An Online Catalogue of Israel Military Products and Israel Army Surplus Store:** 56br; **iStockphoto.com:** Maxim Ahner 64-65 (Background), 66-67 (Background), 68-69 (Background), 70-71 (Background); Johan Axelsson 61br; Jeff Salvant 21br; Duncan Walker 32tr (Confederate), 32tr (Union); **Library Of Congress, Washington, D.C.:** 21cr, 42tr, 67cl; Jame Montgomery Flagg 8cr; **MAVSTAR, ARC Centre of Excellence for Autonomous Systems:** 62tl; **Medicine Hat Miniature Model Association (MHMMA):** Stuart LeCrerar 33; **National Army Museum:** 9bc; **NATO Media Library:** 11tr; **Courtesy of Oshkosh Corporation:** 63br; **PA Photos:** 57t, 58br; AP Photo 61tr; AP Photo / El Paso Times / Mark Lambie 63cr; AP Photo / Ng Han Guan 67cr; AP Photo / Rob Griffith 50br; AP Photo / Vincent Yu 68c; **Panos Pictures:** Paul Smith 59tr; **Photolibrary:** Robert Harding Travel / Guy Thouvenin 15bc; Photononstop / A.J. Cassaigne 50ubl; **Point Blank Solutions, Inc.:** 24r; **Rex Features:** 35br, 46cl; Action Press 52cra; ITV 66bl; Timo Jaakonaho 51tr; Sipa Press

12c, 58tr, 61cr; **Daniel Steger, Lausanne, Switzerland:** 37br; **Still Pictures:** Argus / Hartmut Schwarzbach 60tl; Das Fotoarchiv / Friedrick Stark 57bl; **Saigo Takamori and Okubo Toshimichi:** 39tr; **Courtesy of U.S. Air Force:** Tech. Sgt. Russell E. Cooley IV 34cr; **Courtesy of U.S. Army:** 21cb; SPC Timothy J. Belt 29clb; Cameras in Action 8cb; Spc. Eric E. Hughes 23br; Pfc. Matthew McLaughlin 14tr; Sgt. 1st Class Derrick A. Witherspoon 45cl; **Courtesy of U.S. Navy:** Photographer's Mate 1st Class Brien Aho 39br; Mass Communication Specialist Seaman Christopher L. Clark 39cr; Mass Communication Specialist Seaman Michael Croft 70bl; Mass Communication Specialist 2nd Class Lolita M. Lewis 43tl; Photographer's Mate 2nd Class Daniel J. McLain 34tl; Pfc. C. Warren Peace 25tr; Cpl. Jessica L. Richards 46-47bc; Photographer's Mate 2nd Class Michael Sandberg 28r; Cpl. Robert A. Sturkie 13bl; **The US National Archives and Records Administration:** 56tr; **US Army Natick Soldier RD&E Center:** Sarah Underhill 1, 62cr, 62-63c.

Wall chart: Alamy Images: North Winds Picture Archives (cb); **Corbis:** Michael S. Yamashita (fcr) (cl) (clb) (fclb); **DK Images:** Courtesy of David Edge (fcla); Courtesy of the Gettysburg National Military Park, PA (bc); Tracy Morgan (cla); Courtesy of the Royal Green Jackets Museum, Winchester (crb); Courtesy of the Wallace Collection, London (cl: halberd); **Getty Images:** The Bridgeman Art Library (tr); **Courtesy of U.S. Navy:** Photographer's Mate 2nd Class Michael Sandberg (fbl); **US Army Natick Soldier RD&E Center:** Sarah Underhill (c)

Jacket: Front: Corbis: Pavel Wolberg; EPA: b, Swim Ink 2, LLC: tl; Getty Images: US Air Force – digital version © Science Faction: tc Back: Corbis: Swim Ink 2, LLC: cl; Photolibrary: b.

All other images © Dorling Kindersley
For further information see: **www.dkimages.com**